The Politics of
Teacher Education
Reform

Politics of Education Association

Yearbook Sponsor

The **Politics of Education Association (PEA)** promotes the development and dissemination of research and debate on educational politics and policy. The PEA brings together scholars, practitioners, and policymakers interested in educational governance and politics. The PEA began as a special interest group (SIG) of the American Educational Research Association in 1969. Since 1987, the PEA has sponsored a yearbook focused on seminal issues of educational politics, research, policy, and innovations at local, state, national, and international levels. These yearbooks are designed as both text and references for scholars, students, and practitioners. The annual membership dues are $US25.00 (subject to change). Membership includes a copy of the *Yearbook* and the *Politics of Education Bulletin,* which includes occasional papers on the scholarship in our field. Membership dues should be sent to **Louise Adler, PEA Treasurer, ED 552, Educational Administration, California State University at Fullerton, Fullerton, CA 92634–8000, USA.**

Previous *Yearbooks* and their editors are:

The Politics of Excellence and Choice in Education
William Boyd and Charles Kerchner (1987)

The Politics of Reforming School Administration
Jane Hannaway and Robert Crowson (1988)

Education Policies for the New Century
Douglas Mitchell and Margaret Goetz (1989)

Politics of Curriculum and Testing
Susan Fuhrman and Betty Malen (1990)

The Politics of Urban Education in the United States
James G. Cibulka, Rodney J. Reed, and Kenneth K. Wong (1991)

The New Politics of Race and Gender
Catherine Marshall (1992)

The Politics of Linking Schools and Social Services
Louise Adler and Sid Gardner (1993)

The Study of Educational Politics
Jay D. Scribner and Donald H. Layton (1994)

The Politics of Education and the New Institutionalism:
Reinventing the American School
Robert L. Crowson, William Lowe Boyd, and Hanne B. Mawhinney (1995)

Expertise Versus Responsiveness in Children's Worlds
Maureen McClure and Jane Clark Lindle (1996)

The Politics of Accountability: Educative and International Perspectives
Reynold J. S. Macpherson (1997)

Accuracy or Advocacy: The Politics of Research in Education
Bruce Cooper and E. Vance Randall (1998)

The Politics of Teacher Education Reform

The National Commission **Reform**
on Teaching and America's Future

Edited by
Karen Symms Gallagher
Jerry D. Bailey

Yearbook of the Politics of Education Association

CORWIN PRESS, INC.
A Sage Publications Company
Thousand Oaks, California

For information, address to:

Corwin Press, Inc.
A Sage Publications Company
2455 Teller Road
Thousand Oaks, California 91320
E-mail: order@corwinpress.com

Sage Publications Ltd.
6 Bonhill Street
London EC2A 4PU
United Kingdom

Sage Publications India Pvt. Ltd.
M-32 Market
Greater Kailash I
New Delhi 110 048 India

Printed in the United States of America

ISBN 0-7619-7677-9

ISBN 0-7619-7678-7

Library of Congress Cataloging-in-Publication Data

This book is printed on acid-free paper.

00   01   02   03   04   05   06   10   9   8   7   6   5   4   3   2

Editorial Assistant: Julia Parnell
Typesetter: Rose Tylak
Cover Designer: Oscar Desierto

Contents

Introduction to the Politics
of Teacher Preparation Reform

KAREN SYMMS GALLAGHER
and JERRY D. BAILEY

TO CONFINE AN ANALYSIS of the politics of teacher preparation to a single volume is an impossible task. Our purpose is a more modest one: to examine "an audacious goal" of providing every student in the United States with access to a competent, caring, and qualified teacher. This audacious goal led off the opening pages of *What Matters Most: Teaching for America's Future*, the 1996 report of the National Commission on Teaching & America's Future (NCTAF). Since that time, the commission's reform agenda and call to action have generated conversations and controversies throughout policy-making and education circles. In some states, the commission's work has led once again to increased efforts to change the manner in which beginning teachers are prepared and experienced teachers receive professional development. Soon after the report's release, 12 states applied to become partners with the commission and were accepted. Legislation based on the commission's work has been enacted in more than 20 partner and nonpartner states. The National Governors' Association and the Education Commission of the States include the NCTAF's policy strategies as part of their outreach to state legislatures.

However, at the national level, critics from many quarters have issued policy papers suggesting that the recommendations of the national commission are flawed and ill advised. Proposals to "break the ed school monopoly" and bar education schools from receiving any federal assistance have been issued from the Heritage Foundation, the Progressive Policy Institute, and the Education Leaders Council. Several such critics testified before Congress against proposed legislation based on NCTAF recommendations. Compare this

EDUCATIONAL POLICY, Vol. 14 No. 1, January and March 2000 6-9

reaction to the local level, in the 15,000 school districts in the United States and in the 1,200 schools, colleges, and departments of education in postsecondary institutions, in which the NCTAF's recommendations have largely been ignored or dismissed as irrelevant.

The popular press picked up on the findings from the report and responded accordingly. For example, David Broder's commentary in September 1996 stated,

> What is one to make of this report, "that the current standards for training and hiring teachers are well below the needs of the information-age society and a growing, diverse student body," the comment that "more than 50,000 people who lack the training required for their jobs have entered teaching annually on emergency or substandard licenses. Nearly one-fourth of all secondary teachers do not have even a college minor in their main teaching field." It is instructive to ask what the reaction would be if we were talking, not about schools, but about the nation's airlines, where the business and professional elite of this country spends so much of its time. Suppose a report had been issued last week saying that thousands of unqualified pilots and air controllers were being placed in cockpits and control towers each year. How long would it take the government to stop that practice? Well, you say, lives would be at stake. Believe me, the lives of these children are at stake. If they are not helped to get the survival skills for this modern economy by competent, motivated teachers, their lives are going to be a misery. (p. A19)

Thus, this commission report seems to have captured the attention of a wide range of policy makers, practitioners, and the public.

Some will question our choice of this national report as the basis for an issue on the politics of teacher preparation reform. After all, dozens of reports during the past 50 years have identified the problems in public schools as stemming from incompetent or unqualified teachers and claim that such deficiencies are caused by the shortcomings of teacher education programs. What is different about the NCTAF recommendations?

First, research studies conducted in the past decade have discovered a great deal about effective teaching and learning. Previous reports did not have access to this body of evidence. Second, many reform reports have issued recommendations; caused a few weeks of attention to be paid to schools, students, teachers, and/or achievement; and then disappeared to rest on shelves. The national commission seems to have broken that mold. Not only has the attention to issues of teacher quality continued to attract the interest of policy makers and the public, but legislation like Title II from the Higher Education Act has provided funding for some of the recommendations found in *What Matters Most*. We also believe that previous reports have ignored the weight of evidence that what teachers know and can do makes the crucial difference in what students learn. And the way schools organize the work of teachers makes a big difference in what teachers can accomplish. The commission recommended five major interlocking changes:

- Get serious about standards, for both students and teachers.
- Reinvent teacher preparation and professional development.
- Overhaul teacher recruitment and put qualified teachers in every classroom.
- Encourage and reward teaching knowledge and skill.
- Create schools that are organized for student and teacher success.

Within these five recommendations are 22 specific actions that are systemic in scope. They are based on the premises that school reform can succeed only if it is broad and comprehensive and only if changes are made simultaneously. These premises clearly reflect certain values and beliefs about educational change, the nature of schooling, and the direction required for meaningful student achievement. Such are the topics found in previous editions of the *Politics of Education Yearbook.*

The articles presented in this yearbook speak to the underlying assumptions, research bases, and values found in the recommendations of the national commission. In Part 1, the three articles discuss longtime and persistent issues about teaching, teacher education programs, and public policy making. In the first article, Karen Symms Gallagher and Jerry D. Bailey review the 1910 Flexner report on medical education as a model reform report and an example of strategic philanthropy. The tension between expertise on one hand and full participation in decision making on the other is central to their discussion. Penelope M. Earley reviews the superficial treatment of teacher education policies at the federal level and puts into context the recent initiatives coming from the federal government such as Title II of the 1999 Higher Education Act. Frank B. Murray analyzes issues of accreditation of teacher education programs within higher education institutions and suggests an alternative approach to accreditation that is not based on standards set externally.

In Part 2, we provide two state-level stories that encompass recommendations by the national commission. Both Indiana and Georgia are partnership states with the NCTAF, although the reforms discussed by the authors were in place before the NCTAF released its report. Marilyn M. Scannell and Philip L. Metcalf describe Indiana's autonomous Professional Teaching Standards Board as one example of standards-based reform for teachers. They relate Indiana's experiences with building a structure for the teaching profession to control standards and licensure. Next, Jan S. Kettlewell, Janine A. Kaste, and

Sheila A. Jones tell the story of Georgia's P-16 Initiative. The role of standards in the development of both states' reform efforts is clear.

Part 3 presents the urban school partnership found in Cincinnati, Ohio. Robert J. Yinger and Martha S. Hendricks-Lee detail the development of a pattern language that eventually enabled the University of Cincinnati, the Cincinnati Public Schools, and the Cincinnati Federation of Teachers to form a partnership for both teacher preparation and professional development. The Cincinnati story continues in the next article. Four principal players in the partnership, Arlene Harris Mitchell, Louis A. Castenell, Jr., Martha S. Hendricks-Lee, and Tom Mooney, describe taking the standards developed for the Cincinnati Initiative for Teacher Education and implementing them. The two articles should be read together.

Part 4 has three articles, which cover some of the micropolitics of teacher education. Sally Frost Mason, a dean of liberal arts and sciences, addresses the issue of how schools of education and colleges of arts and sciences should work together, since education students take considerably more courses outside of their education school than they take in the education school. Dennis Thiessen discusses the role of knowledge and the pressing need to make use of what is already known. Richard D. Howard, Randy Hitz, and Larry J. Baker build on a study done earlier about the internal funding of academic units in higher education.

The issue ends with an afterword by Linda Darling-Hammond, staff director of the national commission.

Each article was written to stand alone in discussing the politics of reforming an endeavor that has never enjoyed much regard from the public or members of the teaching profession. We believe, however, that taken as a whole, this yearbook will provide an insightful and introspective story of why teacher quality matters enough to keep it central to all reform efforts.

REFERENCES

Broder, D. (1996, September 18). Teachers as crucial as pilots. *The Washington Post*, p. A19.
National Commission on Teaching & America's Future. (1996). *What matters most: Teaching for America's future*. New York: Author.

Part 1

Issues From the National Arena

The Politics of Teacher Education Reform: Strategic Philanthropy and Public Policy Making

KAREN SYMMS GALLAGHER
and JERRY D. BAILEY

The issue of what appropriate role philanthropic foundations should play in the formation of policies related to the education of professionals is explored. Specifically, the 1910 Flexner report on medical education and the 1996 National Commission on Teaching & America's Future report on teacher education, both financed by Carnegie foundations, are compared and contrasted. The influence of strategic philanthropy in the democratic process has decreased over 90 years, so more public engagement is needed if meaningful changes in practice are to occur.

ALL THINGS CONSIDERED, the American public has never cared much about the education of elementary and secondary teachers. It, however, has always seemed to be fashionable and politically expedient to criticize the preparation of schoolteachers, whether programs are based in the liberal arts, former normal schools, or research universities. Because parents, business leaders, and policy makers have all served "apprenticeships of observation" (Darling-Hammond, 1998, p. 58) as students in the past, they "know how to teach" and have little public appreciation of what it means to be truly prepared for teaching. Teachers themselves are critical of their professional preparation, citing too much theory in pedagogical coursework and not enough real-world, practice-based skills. In the academy, liberal arts and sciences faculty denigrate education schools' faculty, research, students, and curriculum, and even within education schools, many faculty, usually those

EDUCATIONAL POLICY, Vol. 14 No. 1, January and March 2000 11-24
© 2000 Corwin Press, Inc.

in graduate programs, distance themselves from the preparation of new teachers.

Dozens of reports in the past 50 years have identified problems and recommended solutions for fixing what is wrong with public schooling. Eminent scholars like James Bryant Conant (1963) and John Goodlad (1990) have written detailed studies of the preparation of teachers. In general, these reports have been critical of teacher education. Most criticisms center on one of five areas: poor quality of students who want to be teachers, structural deficiencies of preparation programs, duration of preparation programs, placement or sequence of teacher preparation coursework, and clinical training (Lucas, 1997). Many reform reports have come out of commissions that were created to respond to perceived crises. When major reports such as *A Nation Prepared: Teachers for the 21st Century* (Carnegie Forum, 1986) or *Action for Excellence* (Task Force on Education and the Economy, 1983) were issued, their recommendations were often only partially presented to the public and superficially understood. Responses from educators are often defensive ("We are already doing that") or apathetic ("This too shall pass"). An advantage of such documents is that they can call attention to problems by shaping the discourse among the public, practitioners, and policy makers. At the same time, their vulnerability lies in their use by partisan groups as ideological dogma or political slogans, with little widespread understanding of the meaning of the recommendations.

Such, then, is the historical context for *What Matters Most: Teaching for America's Future*, issued by the National Commission on Teaching & America's Future (NCTAF) in September 1996. The Rockefeller Foundation and the Carnegie Corporation of New York funded the work of this commission in 1994. The NCTAF's (1996) mission was "to provide an action agenda for meeting America's educational challenges, connecting the quest for higher student achievement with the need for teachers who are knowledgeable, skillful, and committed to meeting the needs of all students" (NCTAF, 1996, p. i). At the heart of this report is the basic proposition that what teachers know and can do is the most important influence on what students learn. This proposition what separates *What Matters Most* from previous reports. Teacher quality frames the audacious goal of the commission: "By the year 2006, America will provide all students in the country with what should be their educational birthright—access to competent, caring and qualified teachers" (p. vi).

What Matters Most has been compared to the Flexner report, the influential 1910 Carnegie Foundation for the Advancement of Teaching (CFAT) survey of medical education that is widely credited with changing the direction of the American medical profession. Although there are many similarities between teacher education in the 1990s and medical education in the first decades of the 20th century, there are also some major differences. More important for this article is the issue of which role philanthropic foundations should play in the exploration of new directions for public policy, specifically policy development for a prerequisite of democracy such as public education. A dilemma inherent in societies such as the United States is related to this issue: Democracy requires sufficient education and information for all citizens to enable them to participate meaningfully in decisions affecting them, yet specialized knowledge—expertise—has often stood in opposition to universal and equal participation in public affairs. When the public debate is over what kind of public education is appropriate for all students, both expertise and equality of participation are vital to the policies adopted.

PREVIOUS STUDIES OF THE
EDUCATION OF PROFESSIONALS

Philanthropic foundations such as Rockefeller and Carnegie have played critical roles in identifying how the education of various professions in the United States should be structured. Probably the most obvious example is the evolution of medical education. The appearance of the report *Medical Education in the United States and Canada*, written in 1910 by Abraham Flexner, a former high school teacher on staff at the Carnegie Foundation, has been viewed as the catalyst that changed the course of American medical education. The study was commissioned by then-president Henry Pritchett, to demonstrate the Carnegie Foundation's, capacity "to catalyze movement toward the elevated scientific standards" (CFAT mission statement) Pritchett believed institutions of higher education should maintain. The Flexner report was designed to empower and be empowered by an already established drive of the American Medical Association (AMA) to reform medical education. The report's success in bringing about the closure of small, local, proprietary institutions with low standards was also the fulfillment of Pritchett's desire for the Carnegie Foundation to influence important public policy matters.

Lawyers were dazzled (Lagemann, 1989) by the apparent effectiveness of Flexner's (1910) report in closing proprietary schools and advocating a single model of university-based medical education. Although the legal profession was also at a crossroads in the early 20th century, its professional evolution differed from that of physicians. Until the last two decades of the 19th century, American lawyers seemed to have been able to combine statesmanship with their private legal practice. But as the law became more specialized and as corporate law and large law firms began to attract the most prominent members of the bar, the legal profession lost support from the public. In addition, many of the newest immigrants to the United States were entering the legal profession through admission to the growing number of proprietary schools whose standards were low and whose professors were practicing attorneys by day (Lagemann, 1989).

In 1913, Pritchett received a letter from the American Bar Association (ABA) requesting "an investigation . . . into the conditions under which the work of legal education is carried out in this country" (Reed, 1921, p. xviii). Alfred Z. Reed, who was not a lawyer just as Flexner was not a doctor, wrote the resulting study. *Training for the Public Profession of the Law* (1921) was a lengthy review of the divisions that existed between elite corporate lawyers and academic lawyers on one hand and everyday local attorneys who usually served the poor on the other. Unlike Flexner's call for one model of university-based education, Reed recommended different kinds of training for different kinds of practitioners. Although he was critical of the standards of the proprietary schools, he did not recommend their closure.

This was not the message that the ABA leadership wanted. Its committee on legal education, chaired by Elihu Root, who also sat on the CFAT's board of trustees, received a preliminary copy of Reed's (1921) report. The committee repudiated his recommendations, and the final report was delayed for several months. The ABA, which had hoped for "a legal Flexner report," then feared that the Reed report would have the effect of increasing immigrant entrance into the legal profession. In reaction, the previously reluctant membership of the legal education committee recommended that all candidates to the bar graduate from a law school requiring 2 years of collegiate preparation.

Andrew Carnegie, himself an immigrant, died in August 1919, a year before Reed completed his report. Carnegie created the foundation in hopes that it would elevate scientific standards and advance knowledge, thus increasing opportunities for education. He had not envisioned the various Carnegie foundations as directly influencing governance because he believed that an educated citizenry diminished the need for any kind of regulatory structure, be it professional or governmental. The reaction of the elite legal community and members of the foundation's board of trustees to the Reed report showed how different Carnegie's commitment to education and its role in a democratic society was from that of the men whom he appointed to the various boards of his philanthropic foundations. Nonetheless, the publication of two such landmark policy studies established the Carnegie Foundation's leadership role in critiquing and improving standards of professional education.

THE FLEXNER REPORT
ON MEDICAL EDUCATION

In the early 1900s, the legal profession and physicians were at a critical juncture in their development. This juncture was whether they would continue to take their cues almost exclusively from practitioners of their craft or open themselves up to the research and theory of those who inquired into their practice. Elite groups of lawyers and physicians from research universities, corporations, and cities in the northeast region of the United States chose the latter road, away from proprietary schools and control by local practitioners. The Flexner (1910) report has long been recognized as propelling medicine toward a university-based model best represented in the United States at that time by Johns Hopkins University. There are parallels between the context and conduct of medical education in 1910 and teacher education in the 1990s, so it seems appropriate to provide a few details of the Flexner study to understand of what it did indeed recommend.

Many groups involved in the education of physicians in the late 19th and early 20th centuries had come to general agreement as to what was needed. Both the AMA and the Association of American Medical Colleges (AAMC) cooperated with Flexner in his investigations. And, as will be seen, strategic philanthropy from the Rockefeller Institute made many of his recommendations feasible.

Medical Education in the United States and Canada (Flexner, 1910) is divided into two parts. The first part recounts the history of medical education in the United States, describes its existing status, and suggests how it could be improved. The first part is organized into two sections: the deficiencies found in the medical curriculum, facilities, instructional equipment, faculties, and financial resources of the existing medical schools; and the weaknesses and inconsistencies of the system of state board examinations. The second part of the report presents a state-by-state description of each medical school. Included is information on each school's founding, entrance requirements, enrollment, teaching staff, general resources, sources of funds, laboratory facilities, and clinical facilities, as well as the date on which the school was visited by Flexner. At the end of the report, Flexner presents general considerations and recommendations.

Flexner's (1910) report presents data on 155 medical schools, 7 of which were in Canada. Of the 148 in the United States, 116 were considered "regular medical schools" and 32 were considered "sectarian." The sectarian schools included 15 homeopathic, 8 osteopathic, 8 eclectic, and 1 physiomedical. All sectarian schools except two homeopathic schools were proprietary. At the time of Flexner's study, student fees were the primary financial basis for all but 21 of the medical schools. These 21 medical schools, whose income from other sources exceeded income from student fees, were all located in the northeast or midwest regions of the United States and affiliated with institutions of higher education (Bordley & Harvey, 1976).

Among the regular medical schools, those with the largest enrollments were the University of Louisville (Kentucky) with 600 students, Jefferson Medical School in Philadelphia with 591, and the University of Pennsylvania with 546. The sectarian school with the largest enrollment was the American School of Osteopathy in Kirksville, Missouri, with 560 students. Three of these four medical schools were wholly dependent on student fees; Pennsylvania received support from general university funds. Only four private, regular medical schools had endowments sufficient to provide a dependable flow of dollars for medical education: Harvard, $3,327,000; Washington University, St. Louis, $1,500,000; the College of Physicians and Surgeons, New York, $832,000; and Western Reserve, $785,000. Both Yale and Cornell, with very modest endowments for their medical schools, made substantial contributions toward operating expenditures from university general funds (Bordley & Harvey, 1976).

The impact of the Flexner (1910) report was due not only to its revelation of the incompetence of the great majority of American medical schools but also to the uncompromising language used to describe the conditions found in these schools. For instance, the following excerpt describes the curriculum at the University of Louisville, the largest of the American schools, as an example of the general disregard for graduates' competence:

It was a school in which the lecture was everything. Within the brief compass of four months the whole medical lore was unfolded in discourses following one another in bewildering sequence through a succession of long days; and lest the wisdom imparted should exceed the student's power of retention, the lectures were repeated precisely the second year, at the end of which graduation with the degree of Doctor of Medicine was all but automatic. (p. 137)

Flexner (1910) appeared to realize that the popularity of the sectarian branches, particularly homeopathy, was waning, and such approaches could be absorbed by regular medical education or replaced by fields like pharmacology as new scientific breakthroughs occurred. His assessment of the eight eclectic schools was scathing: "without exception filthy and bare." The eight osteopathic schools "fairly reek with commercialism. Their catalogues are a mass of hysterical exaggerations, alike of the earning and of the curative power of osteopathy" (Bordley & Harvey, 1976, p. 192).

He was no less harsh in his criticisms of the majority of the regular medical schools. Flexner (1910) recommended that many of them be abandoned and that others be merged into stronger institutions. He believed that far too many doctors were being produced and that the public would be better served by fewer and better educated medical school graduates. The principal findings of the Flexner report can be summed up in the following five observations. He found an

1. overproduction of uneducated and poorly trained medical practi- tioners;
2. existence of commercial medical schools sustained by fraudulent adver- tising claims and university-affiliated medical schools in which institu- tional commitment was to "educational completeness" rather than finan- cial stability;
3. inadequate instructional methods and facilities, as well as lack of curricu- lar standards;
4. misplaced commitment to educational access rather than to high standards of medical education;
5. lack of adequate hospitals under the complete control of a medical school with sufficient funds to employ clinical teaching faculty.

By 1920, 76 medical schools had gone out of existence, by either ceasing to function or merging with stronger institutions (Goodlad, 1990). This fig- ure represented nearly half of the medical schools that Flexner reviewed 10 years earlier. In 1918, the Council on Medical Education raised its require- ments for admission to medical school to 2 years of college, and within 2 years, 90% of the medical schools accepted this requirement. Also, an increasing number of medical schools were requiring a bachelor's degree for admission (Bordley & Harvey, 1976).

CONTEXT OF
MEDICAL EDUCATION IN 1910

Although the Flexner report was a major factor in awakening the Ameri- can public to the poor quality of medical practitioners' preparation, its publi- cation in 1910 came at a time of many progressive sociopolitical reforms. The report reflected several political agendas: growing influence of fledgling philanthropic foundations and benefactors, concerns over traditional values and emerging conditions of industrial America, and growing recognition of the need for expertise to solve problems of modern society.

Like teacher preparation, medical education had many critics in the first 130 years of the United States' existence. As early as the 1870s, prominent citizens recognized the deplorable state of medical education and were beginning to do something about it. Their efforts were strengthened by the contributions of several wealthy philanthropists and the return to American medical schools of young men who had been trained in the foremost laboratories of Europe. In 1876, representatives of 22 medical schools met to form the Provisional Association of the American Medical Colleges. In 1871, the first university-based medical research laboratory was founded at Harvard. Congress established the National Board of Health in 1879 (Marks & Beatty, 1973).

Hospitals were beginning to assume a new role in the provision of health services and the clinical instruction of medical students. Architects paid more attention to the design of hospitals, especially in recognizing the need to prevent the spread of infectious diseases. The establishment of two hospitals under the control of university medical schools—the University of Pennsylvania in 1874 and the University of Michigan hospital in 1877—signaled a significant commitment to the role of clinical instruction. In hospitals in general, laboratory methods had begun to play a part in clinical diagnoses.

Other scientific advances and practices that moved medical practice as well as medical education in the last decades of the 19th century included Lister's work, multiple international experiments relating microorganisms to human disease, the dissemination of Gregor Mendel's experiments with genetics, and Walter Flemming's work in Germany with cell reproduction. The extant medical literature was organized and systematized by John Shaw Billings in the last two decades of the 19th century so as to become more accessible to researchers and practitioners alike. And last, by 1900, state governments were beginning to show serious interest in medical education.

Such was the landscape in the early 1900s when several editorials in the *Journal of the American Medical Association* called attention to the inferior state of medical education in the United States as compared to that in Europe. Emphasis was placed particularly on the poor quality of clinical training not only for medical students but for medical interns as well. During its annual convention in 1904, the AMA created the Council on Medical Education to replace its Committee on Medical Education. The council had among its responsibilities the annual reporting of the status of medical education to the membership. A few months later, the *Journal* suggested to the council that it direct its attention to the educational requirements for admission to medical schools, the relationship between actual performance of medical schools and their claims in their catalogs, and the access of medical schools to clinical materials used in teaching. The *Journal* also called for more adequate state requirements for medical licensure.

In 1905, the council held a conference in Chicago attended by delegates of most states and territories and by committees from the AAMC. Following the meeting, the council proposed to the AMA House of Delegates that the "ideal standard" for medical education include a high school education with a year's training in several basic sciences as a prerequisite for admission to medical school. This was at a time when less than 10% of the U.S. population attended high school. In addition, a 4-year medical curriculum and a 1-year internship were recommended as a minimum. The council also established a rating system for medical schools, with four categories of A to D. Based on periodic inspections, the council graded the schools and lobbied states not to grant licenses to graduates of D schools. The council also made available a draft of a model bill that states could adopt to license medical practitioners (Bordley & Harvey, 1976).

Perhaps even more important than the AMA's own contribution to the betterment of medical education was the assistance that its Council on Medical Education gave to Flexner in his investigation of American medical schools. The secretary of the council gave Flexner access to materials the council had gathered and accompanied him during his visits to some of the medical schools (Berman, 1983).

When *Medical Education in the United States and Canada* appeared in 1910, a confluence of other critical studies, scientific advances, and previous AMA recommendations served to support and reinforce it. In fact, the AMA and the *Journal* had done much to prepare the medical profession to accept the recommendations made in the Flexner report. Without the AMA, its Council on Medical Education, and the AAMC, Flexner's recommendations would have faced even stiffer initial resistance.

ROLE OF THE CARNEGIE FOUNDATION

When Pritchett sought an opportunity to demonstrate the foundation's capacity to catalyze movement toward elevated scientific standards he believed institutions of higher education should maintain, the reform of medical education seemed a logical and propitious project. The CFAT, established by Andrew Carnegie in 1906, was a professional pension fund that also conducted education studies. Pritchett commissioned the study and put his assistant at the foundation, Flexner, in charge of conducting the investigation.

Although Flexner was not a medical doctor, his brother Dr. Simon Flexner was. Dr. Flexner personally had experienced various models of medical education, as he had gone to medical school at the University of Louisville, several schools in Europe, and Johns Hopkins. Dr. Flexner at the time of his brother's study was at the Rockefeller Institute. He and Dr. William H. Welch of Johns Hopkins University were support staff to Flexner during his inspections of several medical schools and assisted in the writing of the final report (Flexner, 1910).

In Flexner's specifications, the future physician needed first to be well educated. Two years of general education were to be followed by 2 years of medically related subject matter, such as anatomy, and increasing amounts of practical work, and then by 2 years of specialized subject matter and hospital-based practice. Two characteristics of the Flexner report make it a compelling standard for teacher education. First, Flexner set down standards for all medical schools to meet rather than developing educational objectives for students that weak schools could claim they were trying to meet. Second, by gathering data from all 155 medical schools, Flexner was able to cut off claims that he had described only the "bad examples." Not only did nearly half of the medical schools in existence in 1910 close, but those that survived and improved did so with the help of the private sector. In fact, Flexner left the Carnegie Foundation shortly after his report was published and went to the General Education Board of the Rockefeller Institute. He was instrumental in awarding several large grants to Johns Hopkins University hospital and medical school as they strengthened their highly regarded medical education model.

Change may have come without the intervention of financial support from foundations, but with their assistance, medical schools began to receive public money allocated to universities for medical education. Medical education had successfully negotiated a critical juncture to arrive at professional status.

CONTEXT OF TEACHER
EDUCATION IN THE 1990s

Eighty-four years after commissioning the Flexner (1910) report, the Carnegie Corporation of New York and the Rockefeller Foundation collaborated to promote an understanding of what is needed for all students to achieve at higher levels and to establish the standard for all students to have access to high-quality instruction. Although *What Matters Most* (NCTAF, 1996) has been compared to the Flexner report as a document that will catalyze teacher quality and the need for both high-quality teacher preparation and professional development, it seems unrealistic to place so many expectations on a single written report. After all, reports do not implement themselves, as the NCTAF commissioners realized. In fact, the conditions prevalent in medical education in the decades before the Flexner report had as much to do with the changes as the Carnegie Foundation–sponsored study. Still, reading a single report with the breadth and depth that Flexner's study contained provided the public with an understanding of medical education it had not had before.

Are similar conditions in place for teacher education in the 1990s? There are nine times as many institutions preparing teachers today as there were medical schools in 1910; the differences among these 1,300 schools, colleges, and departments of education are vast. Among the differences are those pertaining to their acceptance and integration of the mission, purposes, and standards of the college or university of which they are part. However, many schools of education have met more rigorous standards of quality; more than 300 have created graduate-level programs in partnership with P-12 professional development schools. Elementary and secondary schools have not been standing still either. Thousands have redesigned curriculum and instruction, implemented new programs working with parents, and reshaped professional development to more closely support student performance standards. There are programs for teacher induction, mentoring and peer assistance, and student assessments tied to statewide curriculum frameworks. New standards for certification by the National Board for Professional Teaching Standards have been developed in the past 10 years. The issue now is how to move from these individual disconnected efforts to a coherent system that supports high-quality teaching for every teacher in every school in the United States.

The NCTAF core recommendations address the past criticisms of teaching and teacher education as well as build on the substantial progress already made: Rely on high-quality standards for learning and teaching, reinvent teacher preparation and professional development, recruit qualified teachers for every classroom, encourage and reward knowledge and skill, and recreate schools as learning communities. These core recommendations are strikingly similar to the five principal observations of Flexner (1910). Recognizing that these are not all-new ideas and that previous education reform commissions have failed to implement their agendas, the commission argued for a different strategy. Instead of adopting only those recommendations that favor one group's goals over another, *What Matters Most* calls for a pursuit of all the recommendations together. The report is a "tightly interwoven tapestry. Pulling on a single thread will create a tangle rather than tangible progress" (NCTAF, 1996, p. 116).

This notion of interdependence among the recommendations makes the NCTAF report more comprehensive than Flexner's (1910) study. The reinvention of teacher preparation alone would not raise the level of student achievement in classrooms. As Gallagher (1998) has noted, schools, colleges, and departments of education are but one of the constituent groups that influence the development of quality teaching. Policy makers such as governors, state legislators, and boards of education; professional organizations; parents; teacher educators; and teachers themselves will have to do more to raise learning to new levels. In 1910, the AMA, Flexner, and the Carnegie Foundation focused only on the pipeline to practice. Perhaps if they had believed that the responsibility for agreeing on and improving standards for public health and medical care belonged to everyone in a democratic society, the recurring debates over health care, medical coverage, and control of practice may have been different.

STRATEGIC PHILANTHROPY AND PUBLIC POLICY

A lingering question remains. In the public policy arena, do philanthropic foundations matter the way they did when Andrew Carnegie established the CFAT or the Carnegie Corporation of New York? During the 20th century, both of these foundations helped establish libraries and research councils. They set standards for higher education and secondary schools. They supported research on business and intellectual development. They funded conferences, intellectual exchanges, and media presentations. The Carnegie Corporation financed seminal works by Gunnar Myrdal and John W. Gardner. Through these acts of advancement and diffusion of knowledge and understanding, the leaders of the Carnegie foundations exerted influence over public policy making and shaped the knowledge necessary for enactment of many public policies.

The politics of knowledge creation and dissemination is central to the work of all who are involved in public education. Lagemann (1989) argues that this politics involves three large questions. The first asks which fields of knowledge and which approaches within different fields will be recognized as authoritative and therefore associated with the expertise considered relevant to policy making. The second question centers on enfranchisement and participation in public affairs: How should decisions be made and by whom, the expert or everyone affected by the decision? The third question involves access to the political arena of knowledge creation: Who can gain entrance into the elite groups of knowledge producers?

In his role as philanthropist with a purpose, Carnegie answered these questions by empowering a close circle of colleagues with similar interests, educational backgrounds, knowledge bases, and personalities to become the trustees, officers, and staff of his foundations. In 90 years of operation, the various Carnegie foundations had varying degrees of influence on public policy. Clearly, the Flexner (1910) report allowed a small elite group within the Carnegie Foundation to answer the questions about the future of medical education. Scientists and researchers who worked in research universities that had control over teaching hospitals would determine the knowledge base of medical practice. Clinical training under the guidance of medical faculty would develop the necessary knowledge and skills in physicians before they practiced on their own. A physician would have both a general education and the specialized knowledge of sciences relevant to medicine. Quality of the practitioner would be more important than popular access to medical education and production of large numbers of practitioners. Such were the answers provided by Flexner and the few men from the medical profession in 1910.

Since World War II, the Carnegie foundations as well as other philanthropic foundations have relied heavily on commissions rather than individuals to explore new directions for public policy. Commissions are more appropriate for dramatizing an issue, resolving political differences, and reassuring the public that questions are being thoughtfully considered. But this trend is problematic in terms of its consequences for American politics and education. As the debates over public schooling have illustrated in the past two decades, commissions supported by the Carnegie foundations or Rockefeller or the Ford Foundation have effected policies and legislation. However, the process of "commissioning" debate over defining public education, its role in our society, and the standards of achievement for all students may have contributed to a decline in universal participation in the rituals of democracy. Although the efficiency of elite commissions for recommending strategies for educational problems is evident, such strategic philanthropic influence is not the same as the more demanding democratic process.

The members and staff of the NCTAF evidenced some appreciation of this dilemma in how they chose to implement their action plan. A call for state partners to work with the commission was issued in late fall of 1996; by early spring of 1997, the NCTAF had accepted 12 state applications. The state applications included endorsements by governors, state legislative leadership, and leaders from both the P-12 and higher education communities.

In seeking to work with the commission, each state partnership agreed to identify a diverse state policy council whose members would oversee an inventory of conditions of teaching in their state and develop an action plan based on the recommendations of the NCTAF and the results of the state inventory. This is not the usual call to action of so many previous commissions. The NCTAF and the two supporting philanthropic foundations seem to have realized that until local and state constituents get involved in the CFAT's mission of "advancement and diffusion of knowledge and understanding" about teacher quality, expertise alone will again fail to promote citizen involvement in public schooling and its role in a democratic society.

REFERENCES

Berman, E. H. (1983). *The influence of Carnegie, Ford, and Rockefeller Foundation on American public policy: The ideology of philanthropy.* Albany: State University of New York Press.

Bordley, J., & Harvey, A. M. (1976). *Two centuries of American medicine.* Philadelphia: W. B. Saunders.

Carnegie Forum on Education and the Economy. (1986). *A nation prepared: Teachers for the 21st century. Report of the task force on teaching as a profession.* New York: Carnegie Corporation.

Conant, J. B. (1963). *The education of American teachers.* New York: McGraw-Hill.

Darling-Hammond, L. (1998). Afterword: Building capacity for *What matters most.* In M. E. Dilworth (Ed.), *Of course it matters: Putting the national commission report into action* (pp. 55-62). Washington, DC: ERIC Clearinghouse on Teaching and Teacher Education; American Association of Colleges for Teacher Education.

Flexner, A. (1910). *Medical education in the United States and Canada.* Carnegie Forum on Education and the Economy Bulletin No. 4.

Gallagher, K. S. (1998). Audacious goal or déjà vu? In M. E. Dilworth (Ed.), *Of course it matters: Putting the national commission report into action* (pp. 13-24). Washington, DC: ERIC Clearinghouse on Teaching and Teacher Education; American Association of Colleges for Teacher Education.

Goodlad, J. I. (1990). *Teachers for our nation's schools.* San Francisco: Jossey-Bass.

Lagemann, E. C. (1989). *The politics of knowledge: The Carnegie Corporation, philanthropy and public policy.* Chicago: University of Chicago Press.

Lucas, C. J. (1997). *Teacher education in America.* New York: St. Martin's.

Marks, G., & Beatty, W. K. (1973). *The story of medicine in America.* New York: Scribner.

National Commission on Teaching & America's Future. (1996). *What matters most: Teaching for America's future.* New York: Author.

Reed, A. Z. (1921). *Training for the public profession of the law.* Carnegie Forum on Education and the Environment Bulletin No. 15.

Task Force on Education and the Economy. (1983). *Action for excellence.* Education Commission of the States. Denver, CO.

Finding the Culprit: Federal Policy and Teacher Education

PENELOPE M. EARLEY

Attention to teacher preparation has long been part of the federal portfolio of programs. This article reviews federal teacher education policy in the second half of the 20th century and concludes that resulting legislation generally has been driven by a need to identify a culprit when schools do not meet public expectations. This framework is used to consider reauthorization of the Higher Education Act in 1998 and the impact on that reauthorization of the National Commission on Teaching & America's Future. The effect of policies based on competition as a strategy to improve teacher education is considered.

THE FEDERAL GOVERNMENT is primarily a silent junior partner in the development of teacher education policy, with states and institutions of higher education having greater and more consistent influence on the teacher preparation system (Earley & Schneider, 1996; Jordan & Borkow, 1984). Nevertheless, when the federal partner speaks through legislation or executive branch regulation, its voice is loud and its actions can be aggressive. In this article, a framework to characterize federal teacher education policy from the late 1950s to 1999 is presented, with particular attention to reauthorization of the Higher Education Act (HEA) and the impact of the National Commission on Teaching & America's Future (NCTAF) as a catalyst for federal action.

Catalysts by definition lead to a transformation, but not all view the resulting change as positive. Such was the case with the NCTAF (1996) report *What Matters Most: Teaching for America's Future.* Responding to the NCTAF agenda, critics such as Ballou and Podgursky (1997, 1998) and Ballou and Soler (1998) argued that the NCTAF recommendations would do

EDUCATIONAL POLICY, Vol. 14 No. 1, January and March 2000 25-39
© 2000 Corwin Press, Inc.

little to alleviate teacher shortages or improve their preparation and that the commission's recommendations for more stringent regulation of educator preparation and licensure were wrong headed. As media attention to the report declined, negative reactions to the NCTAF agenda subsided, but criticisms of teacher education did not ("Better Schools," 1998; Burd, 1998; Innerst, 1998; Mathews, 1999; Thomas B. Fordham Foundation, 1999). The NCTAF recommendations, contrary points of view by commission critics, and residual blame directed to teacher preparation programs framed discussion of teacher education during reauthorization of the HEA and subsequent enactment of federal accountability legislation as part of Title II of that act.

Following review of, and observations on, the education accountability requirements in the HEA, a policy dilemma for teacher education is posed and considered: Will the market approach to education policy currently enjoying favor with federal and state decision makers result in expected outcomes, or are policies based on a market framework at odds with a teacher education system that prepares a workforce for public schools?

FEDERAL ATTENTION TO TEACHER EDUCATION: ADJUNCT OR CULPRIT?

Federal interest in teachers and their preparation dates to the late 19th and early 20th centuries; however, it was not until after World War II that teacher education began to appear somewhat routinely on the federal agenda (Earley & Schneider, 1996). Unlike major, sustained federal education initiatives—such as compensatory education, student financial assistance to attend college, or support for programs to serve children and youth with special needs—teacher education's legislative place may be characterized as an adjunct to other programs or the culprit when schools do not meet public expectations.

Adjunct

Stedman (1996, 1998) notes that references to initial teacher preparation and continuing professional development show up in a number of federal programs to assist elementary and secondary schools. Although the U.S. Department of Education is the primary source of these authorities in terms of annual appropriations and number of programs, a 1999 study by the General Accounting Office (GAO) revealed that, in fact, 13 federal agencies now administer 87 separate programs that directly or indirectly make awards for teacher education or professional development (Shaul, 1999). It is interesting that 42 of the agencies listed in the GAO report that claim they support teacher education cannot pinpoint how much they spend on it. Nevertheless, with 48% of agencies reporting that they are unsure of their teacher education expenditures, the GAO estimates that the federal government will spend in the range of $1.5 billion in FY 1999 on initial teacher preparation or continuing professional development. This is serious money, but money does not tell the whole story. The GAO survey on which the study was based asked agency officials if programs they administer support teacher education exclusively, significantly, or not significantly. Twelve programs are categorized as exclusively supporting teacher preparation, yet only part of one, the partnership component of the Teacher Quality Enhancement Grants (HEA, Title II), could be realistically described as a program to support systemic changes in teacher preparation, and its FY 1999 funding is less than $35 million. The other programs are narrowly focused, and teacher education or professional development is actually an instrument to achieve another, broader purpose.

The multi-billion-dollar Elementary and Secondary Education Act (ESEA) (1994) presents an example of how teacher education is imbedded in a larger authority as an enabling rather than transforming element. Within it are funds to provide professional development for teachers who work with Title I or limited-English-proficient children and for those teaching in particular content areas. The manner in which teacher education is imbedded in a larger authority is illustrated by the legislative purpose for the Eisenhower Professional Development Program. Pursuant to describing grant provisions in the Eisenhower program, congressional concerns and priorities are outlined in findings (ESEA, Title II, Sec. 2001). These include supporting professional development in discipline-based knowledge and subject-specific pedagogy to help achieve national education goals related to student achievement. The clear intent of the law is to use teacher professional development to change characteristics and skills of particular educators, not to transform the nature of teacher preparation in a fundamental way.

Delivering federal funds for teacher education and continuing professional development is no more consistent than the attendant policy objectives. In certain cases, professional development funds flow through a state higher or K-12 education agency, whereas in others, they are administered by a federal unit. The consequence of this adjunct status within a number of separate federal categorical programs is a patchwork of segmented efforts that individually may have only modest impact on a limited population of teachers. Hill (1999) observes that the fragmentation of the ESEA led to a focus on programs rather than the broader issue of school reform. Thus, in the case of the ESEA, teacher education is in a double bind: It is supplemental rather than central to a large, splintered federal program that by its structure may undermine systemic reform efforts (Phillips & Kanstoroom, 1999).

Culprit

When citizens and policy makers are unhappy with schools, they often look for a place to assign blame. Labaree (1996) suggests that it is always open season on teacher education, but Lucas (1997) observes that in the late 1950s and early 1960s, attacks on educator preparation were especially forceful. Although the policy context of 40 years ago and today differs, criticisms of teacher education then and now and the policy community's response are similar in many ways.

Following World War II, it was assumed that schools would help the nation fight the cold war, win the space race, and secure America's place in a global economy (Education Commission of the States, 1999; Lucas, 1997). During this postwar period, the teacher education curriculum was scrutinized when the United States appeared to lag behind other nations in scientific achievement. Guilt was directed to teacher preparation programs because it was believed they included too much emphasis on teaching methods and too little on content. In a study of the history of teacher education reform, Lucas (1997) details critiques of teacher education in the 1960s. The complaints included James Koerner's stance that teacher education lacked the credentials to be considered an academic discipline, a message echoed by then-director of the Center for Teacher Education at the University of Chicago John Goodlad. This was followed by *The Education of American Teachers*, in which Conant rejected the use of state licensure requirements as a lever for increasing the number of teaching methods in undergraduate preparation programs and recommended instead that new teachers' performance be evaluated by experienced educators (Lucas, 1997).

This opposition to the teacher education curriculum was raised during a period of postwar population growth, and lawmakers were faced with the more immediate need to find strategies to recruit individuals into teaching, especially in high-need urban schools. One response was authorization of the National Teacher Corps program in 1965 (Jordan & Borkow, 1984). Created in a period when reformers were searching for culprits to account for the nation's slow entry into the space race, manpower concerns were more pressing, and the Teacher Corps was initially authorized with a focus to recruit, prepare, and place teachers in schools with high populations of disadvantaged children and youth. Although commentators at the time may have expected that changes in the teacher education curriculum prompted through programs such as Teacher Corps would purge it of irreverent pedagogical instruction, it can be argued that the result was to the contrary. Federal grants through this program, coupled with small federal investments in a teaching and learning research agenda, led to development and acceptance of a knowledge base for teacher education and greater legitimacy of the teacher education curriculum. Yet, like other federal teacher education initiatives, Teacher Corps' direct reach was limited. Roughly 100 institutions received Teacher Corps grants, and its highest appropriation level—in 1973—was $37.5 million, or less than one half of 1% of the appropriations for education and training in that fiscal year. Teacher Corps was repealed in 1981 as part of the Omnibus Budget Reconciliation Act (Earley & Schneider, 1996).

During the 1980s, the federal government's attention to teacher education generally was limited to modest appropriations for professional development in legislation targeted to elementary and secondary schools and children. As noted above, in these cases, teacher education was treated as a useful, but not always essential, appendage to laws designed to serve a broader purpose. Critics of teacher education were muted but not silent, and two examples of attempts to legislate by culprit emerged during the 98th and 99th Congresses. The first was a bill introduced by then-Senator Edward Zorinsky to establish a commission to investigate teacher education in the United States (S. J. Res. 138, 1983). The legislation, which was introduced as a resolution of the Senate but never passed, would have charged the proposed commission to consider the proper balance between instruction in teaching methods and subject matter, the use of "psychological techniques unrelated to academic content in colleges of education" (p. 5), and methods to prepare teachers and their effectiveness. Shortly thereafter, then-Representative Ron Wyden of Oregon introduced H.R. 937 (Teacher Warranty Act, 1985), an amendment to the HEA that would require any institutions that prepare teachers and enroll students receiving federal financial assistance to offer a warranty plan to assist the new teacher during his or her first 2 years of teaching. The Teacher Warranty Act was modified to direct the U.S. Department of Education to study the idea of teacher quality assurance programs and make the information available on request.

Commentaries on the nature of teacher preparation and policy responses during the previous 40 years are helpful reminders that much of the conversation has focused on the content of the curriculum for teachers, who sets that curriculum, and to what extent and by whom it should be regulated. Federal responses to these issues consistently fall into adjunct or culprit reactions, with the need for collegiate-based teacher education programs to build their capacity to meet competing government program expectations rarely considered. It was not surprising when scrutiny of teacher education increased in the mid-1990s that claims about its utility and how to improve it were quite similar to those of the previous 40 years.

ENACTMENT OF 1998 HIGHER
EDUCATION AMENDMENTS

The NCTAF report was an important contribution to the policy agenda in the mid-1990s for several reasons. It consolidated a number of recommendations to refashion teacher education that had been discussed in various venues for several years (e.g., Carnegie Forum on Education and the Economy, 1986; Holmes Group, 1986, 1990, 1995; National Commission for Excellence in Teacher Education, 1985) into one document and bolstered the recommendations with a strong research base. In addition, the commission itself included influential elected officials, as well as education leaders from higher education and K-12 schools, which provided an important political base. The release of the report in 1996 generated considerable media attention—at least for a report on teacher education (Applebome, 1996; Broder, 1996; Sanchez, 1996; Whitmire, 1996). This quickly drew contrary responses from various quarters, such as Ballou and Podgursky (1997, 1998), who argued that the entire report and its assumptions were flawed.

There is no question that the NCTAF report and commentary about it influenced congressional consideration of the HEA in 1997 and 1998. The interesting issue is which parts of the NCTAF agenda resonated with federal policy makers. A review of the statements by congressional leaders, President Clinton, and Education Secretary Riley indicate that policy makers had honed the message to five relatively familiar issues: (a) more people must be recruited into teaching, (b) teachers are not well prepared in the subjects they are expected to teach, (c) teacher education is disconnected from the needs of K-12 schools and from collegiate arts and sciences units, (d) the regulation of teacher preparation and licensure works against teacher quality, and (e) presidents of institutions of higher education with teacher education programs pay little attention to these units (Burd, 1998; Clinton, 1998; Jeffords, 1998; Quality Teacher in Every Classroom Act, 1997). With this backdrop of NCTAF recommendations, contrary opinions and interest among federal officials in teaching reauthorization of the HEA began.

The HEA and Teacher Education

The HEA was first enacted during the 1960s as a vehicle to help needy college students attend institutions of higher learning through a system of federal grants and loans. For nearly 40 years, teacher education initiatives were placed in Title V of the act, a title that became the home for many very small programs that rarely were funded and often were only indirectly connected to the preparation of educators.

As the 105th Congress considered which kinds of programs it would include in the 1998 Higher Education Amendments, lawmakers agreed that Title V should be streamlined and that unfunded programs would no longer be kept on the books. With that clean-slate approach in mind, Congress began to develop amendments to the HEA that would result in its reauthorization for another 5 years. Although most congressional attention was directed to the student financial aid components found in the HEA, Title IV, there was an unusual amount of interest in how the federal government might leverage changes in teacher education.

Interest in ways to revise HEA Title V was not limited to Congress. Many education organizations as well as the U.S. Department of Education believed that concern about teacher education as expressed by the NCTAF and others dictated a new federal investment in educator recruitment and preparation. Moving on parallel but independent tracks, a coalition of higher education organizations, the U.S. Department of Education, and members of Congress developed recommendations for new federal programs to enhance teaching (Earley, 1998). In addition, a number of think tanks, such as the Progressive Policy Institute, called for Congress to address what they termed shortcomings in teacher preparation (Ballou & Soler, 1998). Although proposals from these varied groups differed in terms of legislative details, there was general agreement that any support for collegiate-based teacher education should be linked to institutional partnerships with K-12 schools and that a teacher recruitment section should be included (Stedman, 1998).

The teacher education provisions in the HEA turned out to be extremely controversial. President Clinton (1998), drawing on findings in the NCTAF report, expressed alarm about a possible shortage of teachers. Ballou and Podgursky (1997) and Ballou and Soler (1998) countered that deregulation of teacher preparation and licensure would allow market forces to resolve supply and demand needs. Although the Clinton administration had showed willingness to accept the market strategy of alternative teacher preparation programs as one way to increase the teaching force (Riley, 1999), it was not prepared to turn teacher recruitment into uncharted free-market waters. Instead, the U.S. Department of Education recommended creation of a new teacher recruitment initiative and, in doing so, subsuming an existing Minority Teacher Recruitment program. This was at odds with a proposal from a coalition of higher education associations that wanted any new recruitment program to target persons of color. As policy makers were considering the need for new teachers, the media began reporting dismal news about the scores of potential teachers on a new Massachusetts licensure exam (Laitsch, 1998). This, coupled with information that many states were turning a blind eye to the out-of-field placement of teachers (Ingersoll, 1999), placed decision makers in the position of worrying about teacher recruitment—and the accompanying matter of whether to focus efforts on attracting minority candidates—or searching for and holding accountable the culprits for poor licensure exam performance and inappropriate employment placements. Because much oversight of teacher education is vested in state governments, members of Congress also had to grapple with how far the federal government could tread into areas of authority held by states.

The most vocal advocates for far-reaching accountability provisions in the HEA were New Mexico Senator Jeff Bingaman and California Congressman George Miller. Troubled that the least qualified teachers were being placed in economically disadvantaged California schools, Miller accused collegiate-based teacher education programs of "perpetrating a fraud on the public because they are graduating teachers who aren't prepared to teach" (Burd, 1998, p. A46). The solution, Miller offered, was to cut aid to students in teacher education programs if a federally set percentage of students did not pass the state licensure exam. Although California has no such examination for all teachers, Representative Miller remained a firm proponent of this plan. He was joined by Senator Bingaman, who recommended adding a caveat that if an institution had accreditation through the National Council for Accreditation of Teacher Education (NCATE), their students would not be held to the federally established pass rate on the state licensure examination (Quality Teacher in Every Classroom Act, 1997). These proposals had the effect of galvanizing the higher education community. Terry Hartle (1998) of the American Council on Education, testifying before the Senate Labor and Human Resources Committee on behalf of 18 higher education associations, countered that the Bingaman and Miller proposals were seriously flawed. He cautioned that the proposals would lead to federalization of teacher testing, licensure, and program accreditation; would have an adverse impact on minority teacher recruitment; and would have little impact on the quality of new teachers. A less skeptical perspective was offered by Kati Haycock (1998) of the Education Trust. Haycock urged the Senate to impose a 75% licensure examination pass rate for federal financial aid eligibility, although she did not endorse the notion that the provision should be waived if an institution holds NCATE accreditation. Senator Bingaman and Congressman Miller ultimately dropped their proposal to link student aid to licensure exam performance but persuaded congressional colleagues that other accountability measures be included in the HEA.

Using components from the various teacher education legislative proposals, including new accountability language from Senator Bingaman and Representative Miller, the Senate and House education committees constructed separate bills that ultimately were passed by their respective bodies. Because the House and Senate teacher education provisions were significantly differ-ent, a final bill was developed in a conference committee and passed by both chambers in late September. On October 7, the HEA amendments were signed into law by President Clinton. Certain teacher education provisions in the HEA were enacted in response to assertions made and believed that teacher education is a culprit in school reform failures. Yet, at the same time, legislators included scholarship proposals for students to enroll in teacher education programs as a strategy to meet an expected demand for new teachers.

The teacher education provisions, which were placed in a new Title II of the law, authorized programs to recruit persons into teaching, support higher education and K-12 school partnership arrangements for their preparation, and gather data on the teacher education system in the United States as a way to hold it accountable for the quality of educators who enter K-12 schools. Title II is divided into two sections: categorical programs for partnerships and states and mandatory accountability requirements for states and institu-tions of higher education.

Categorical programs supported through Title II fund partnerships, state initiatives, and teacher recruitment. Forty-five percent of Title II's annual appropriation is for K-16 partnerships, 45% is for state awards, and 10% is reserved for teacher recruitment, with only states or partnerships that qualify for other Title II awards eligible to apply for these funds. Both states and part-nerships must provide in-kind or matching funds and must keep administra-tive costs below 2%. Partnership grants are for 5 years and state grants for 3. They are one-time awards. Title II received an appropriation of $75 million for FY 1999—an amount that, like Teacher Corps in 1973, is half of 1% of the appropriation for education—allowing the Department of Education to launch a grant competition that funded 25 partnerships and 24 states. The partnership programs must link their activities to improving student perform-ance, and states must use their funds to hold colleges and universities accountable for the teachers they prepare or to support alternative routes to licensure.

Teacher Education Accountability

The accountability provisions initiated by Senator Bingaman and Repre-sentative Miller are mandatory but unfunded. All states and colleges or uni-versities that directly or indirectly receive any federal dollars through the HEA must provide the secretary of education with data on teacher prepara-tion standards and licensure procedures. Appreciating that the data collection would require gathering information from states with very different teacher education systems, the National Center for Education Statistics (NCES) was directed to develop key definitions and a uniform reporting method for data required in the HEA, Title II. This must be done in consultation with representatives from higher education and states, and NCES appointed a consultative committee of educators and state officials to help with the task (P. Forgione, Jr., personal communication, January 13, 1999). In addition, the government solicited input through its Web site and a series of focus group meetings.

Accountability provisions in the HEA are enumerated in Title II, Section 207, of the act. They require that data be collected and compiled into institutional and state report cards to be used as indicators of the health of the teacher preparation enterprise. Colleges and universities with teacher preparation programs must provide the state education agency with information on pass rates of their students for each required licensure assessment and make these same data available to the public. In addition, institutions of higher education must report the number of students in the teacher preparation program, faculty-to-student ratio, and average number of hours of supervised practice teaching required. Finally, they must indicate if they are approved or accredited by the state and if the state has designated them as low performing. A fine of up to $25,000 may be imposed by the U.S. Department of Education for noncompliance.

State governments through the agency with authority for teacher licensure or program approval also have a significant reporting burden. They must send the U.S. Department of Education (a) the information they receive from institutions of higher education; (b) a description of licensure requirements and the extent to which K-12 standards and teacher licensure requirements are aligned; (c) the percentage of teaching candidates who passed each required teaching license examination; (d) the pass rate scores on these exams disaggregated by education school, college, or program; (e) the number of licensure waivers granted each year, disaggregated by low- and high-poverty schools; (f) a description of alternate routes to teaching and the percentage of teachers licensed through such routes; (g) the criteria used by the state to evaluate or approve education schools, colleges, or programs; and (h) the name of any institution denied state program approval. All of these data are to be used by the U.S. Department of Education to compile a report card on teacher education that must be transmitted by the secretary to Congress.

Although Representative Miller and Senator Bingaman hoped to deny financial aid to students in teacher education programs with pass rates on licensure exams below a federally set level, only a modified version of their original suggestion was incorporated into Title II. States must have in place a process to identify and assist low-performing education schools, colleges, or programs. If a teacher education unit ultimately loses program approval or state funding for its teacher preparation program due to poor performance, it will not be eligible to receive federal professional development funds, and students in its program will not be eligible for federal student aid (Higher Education Amendments, 1998).

Efforts of the NCTAF and others notwithstanding, recent federal attention to teacher education policy was predicated on identifying and then holding accountable an assumed culprit. Unfunded mandates by the federal government send a punitive message to those who must comply. Although parts of HEA Title II support K-16 partnerships, which one might argue could be used to address accountability requirements, the federal investment is very small, and only a limited number of partnerships will receive grants. Moreover, there has been no attempt to address the existing fragmented approach to federal policy with regard to teacher education and professional development.

POLICY DILEMMA AND
ALTERNATIVE FRAMEWORK

Markets as an Education Policy Framework

Johnson (1999) asserts that the value-laden nature of education research provides policy makers with a resource to further their own political agendas, a perspective echoed by Randall, Cooper, and Hite (1999). As such, data and evidence used in the policy process will have several levels of bias: that embedded in the data or evidence itself, bias associated with analysis, and the biases of those in the policy world who use the information. For policy in teacher education, there is a further intricacy. That is, the potential disconnect between the policy framework employed and the nature and structure of teaching and teacher preparation in the United States. At the heart of this quandary is the conflict between a market approach to education policy making and the values associated with preparing teachers for work in what is primarily a public venture, K-12 schools. Labaree (1997) points out that historically, citizens have had competing goals for education: preparing citizens for a democracy, preparing workers to strengthen the economy, and preparing individuals to compete for social positions (p. 39). He points out that the first two of these are public goods, whereas the latter is a private good. This creates tension between democratic politics and capitalist markets that leads to "ambivalent goals and muddled outcomes" (p. 41). Because teaching is primarily a public enterprise established to promote the common good, market approaches to school reform and public policy are anathematic to the core values of teaching.

It is quite clear that today, a market framework dominates the manner in which decision makers of all political stripes consider education reform. This technique "define[s] its essence through market mechanisms" (Cibulka, 1999, p. 204) and finds comfort in conversations about standardizing education and imposing sanctions on those who do not or cannot conform. It is the framework used by the Progressive Policy Institute (Rotherham, 1999) as well as Secretary Riley (1999) in structuring proposals for the forthcoming reauthorization of the ESEA. Contrasting the values that stimulated creation of the American public school system with this contemporary policy dialogue, an essay published by the Education Commission of the States (1999) notes,

The current move toward decentralization is based on the desire to create an education system based on private or quasi-private markets. As Chubb and Moe argue, it is an effort to replace politics with markets. As such, it is an effort to create an anti-politics of education where consumer choice rather than political interaction defines the education system. (p. 18)

Pushing this concept of markets further, Stone (1997) suggests that in a market approach, "society is viewed as a collection of autonomous, rational decision makers who have no community life" (p. 9), and therefore general welfare becomes nothing more than the sum of "all individuals pursuing their self-interest" (p. 22). Applying a feminist perspective to policy development, Marshall (1999) argues that market viewpoints are anchored in patriarchal traditions that "determine whether a problem becomes part of public discourse" (p. 64). Consequently, alternative ways of conceptualizing a policy question, applying evidence, conducting analysis, and developing recommendations are silenced by the nature of the policy design as well as its substance and the values undergirding it.

Markets, Teachers, and Teacher Education

If there is to be a connection between government's public policy agenda and practices and behaviors in schools, we must attend to the consequences of policy on educational institutions (Cohen & Spillane, 1994). It is this connection that has been absent in federal teacher education initiatives. A market policy lens is based on competition, choice, winners and losers, and finding culprits. Yet, teachers must assume that all children can learn, so there cannot be winners and losers. Market policies applied to public education are at odds with collaboration and cooperative approaches to teaching and learning. An extensive body of literature attests to increases in performance and self-confidence among students engaged in carefully constructed cooperative learning situations when compared with students in traditional classes (e.g.,

Austin, 1997; Johnson, 1993, 1994; Zoltan, 1997). Paradoxically, the HEA Title II categorical programs encourage institutions of higher education to form collaborative partnerships across academic disciplines and with K-12 schools for the purpose of preparing new teachers and offering professional development for career educators. However, under the market approach being used in education policy and reflected in the accountability sections of the same law, teachers and those who design and administer their preparation programs must have as a primary concern competition, being a winner not a loser, and certainly not being cast as a culprit. The consequence of these pressures is the domestication of teachers,[1] perpetuating their role as semiskilled workers (Ingersoll, 1999) and frustrating efforts for teaching to truly be professional work.

CONCLUSION

Accountability as demonstrated in Title II, Section 207, of the HEA is the current mantra of state and federal policy makers. Demands for accountability lead to a search for culprits, and the teacher education system has again been fingered as the responsible party. Decision makers have adopted a market approach to refashioning teacher education without attention to the disconnect between this framework and the characteristics of teachers and the nature of their work. Markets do not promote public discourse; they assume that knowledge and information should not be shared with other professionals—their competitors. This approach leads to the compartmentalization of knowledge and methods of inquiry as well as the isolation of individual educators. Until the teacher education policy dialogue is reframed to take into consideration that schools are public institutions and have a commitment to promoting the common good, teachers and those engaged in teacher preparation again will be designated the culprits when market approaches fail.

NOTE

1. I owe this wonderfully descriptive phrase to Diane Waff, a teacher in the Philadelphia Public Schools.

REFERENCES

Applebome, P. (1996, September 13). Education panel sees deep flaws in training of nation's teachers. *The New York Times*, pp. A1, A26.
Austin, J. D. (1997). Integrated mathematics interfaced with science. *School Science and Mathematics*, 97(1), 45-49.
Ballou, D., & Podgursky, M. (1997). Reforming teacher recruitment: A critical appraisal of the recommendations of the National Commission on Teaching and America's Future. *Government Union Review*, 17(1), 1-51.

Ballou, D., & Podgursky, M. (1998). The case against teacher certification. *The Public Interest, 132*, 17-29.

Ballou, D., & Soler, S. (1998, February). *Addressing the looming teacher crunch* (Policy Briefing). Washington, DC: Progressive Policy Institute.

Better schools for teachers means better teachers for kids. (1998, April 29). *USA Today*, p. A12.

Broder, D. (1996, September 18). Teacher crisis: From bad to worse. *New York Post*, p. 25.

Burd, S. (1998, April 24). Liberal Democrat is unlikely foe of teacher-education programs. *Chronicle of Higher Education*, p. A46.

Carnegie Forum on Education and the Economy. (1986). *A nation prepared: Teachers for the 21st century*. Washington, DC: Author.

Cibulka, J. G. (1999). Moving toward an accountable system of K-12 education: Alternative approaches and challenges. In G. J. Cizek (Ed.), *Handbook of educational policy* (pp. 183-211). San Diego, CA: Academic Press.

Clinton, W. J. (1998, January). *The state of the union*. Washington, DC: The White House.

Cohen, D. K., & Spillane, J. P. (1994). Policy and practice: The relations between governance and instruction. In N. Cobb (Ed.), *The future of education perspectives on national standards in America* (pp. 109-156). New York: College Entrance Examination Board.

Earley, P. M. (1998, October). *Teacher quality enhancement grants for state and partnerships: HEA, Title II* (AACTE Issue Paper). Washington, DC: American Association of Colleges for Teacher Education.

Earley, P. M., & Schneider, E. J. (1996). Federal policy and teacher education. In J. Sikula, T. J. Buttery, & E. Guyton (Eds.), *Handbook of research on teacher education* (2nd ed., pp. 306-319). New York: Simon, Schuster Macmillan.

Education Commission of the States. (1999). *The invisible hand of ideology perspectives from the history of school governance*. Denver, CO: Author.

Elementary and Secondary Education Act of 1994, Pub. L. No. 103-382, 20 U.S.C. § 6301-8962.

Hartle, T. W. (1998, May 7). *Testimony to the Committee on Labor and Human Resources*. Washington, DC: U.S. Senate.

Haycock, K. (1998, May 7). *Testimony to the Committee on Labor and Human Resources*. Washington, DC: U.S. Senate.

Higher Education Amendments of 1998 Conference Report to Accompany H.R. 6. 105th Congress, 2nd Sess. (1998, September 25).

Hill, P. T. (1999). Getting it right the eighth time: Reinventing the federal role. In M. Kanstoroom & C. E. Finn, Jr. (Eds.), *New directions* (pp. 147-170). Washington, DC: Thomas B. Fordham Foundation.

Holmes Group. (1986). *Tomorrow's teachers*. East Lansing, MI: Author.

Holmes Group. (1990). *Tomorrow's schools*. East Lansing, MI: Author.

Holmes Group. (1995). *Tomorrow's schools of education*. East Lansing, MI: Author.

Ingersoll, R. L. (1999). The problem of underqualified teachers in American secondary schools. *Educational Researcher, 28*(2), 26-37.

Innerset, C. (1998, May 8). Schools of education seen as failing. *Washington Times* [Online]. Available: http://washtimes.com/culture/culture1.html

Jeffords, J. (1998, May 7). *Opening statement: Hearing on better teachers for today's classrooms*. Washington, DC: U.S. Senate Committee on Labor and Human Resources.

Johnson, B. L., Jr. (1999). The politics of research-information use in the education policy arena. *Educational Policy, 13*(1), 23-36.

Johnson, D. W. (1993). Impact of cooperative and individualistic learning on high-ability students' achievement, self-esteem, and social acceptance. *Journal of Social Psychology, 133*(6), 839-844.

Johnson, D. W. (1994). *Cooperative learning in the classroom*. Alexandria, VA: Association for Supervision and Curriculum Development.

Jordan, K. F., & Borkow, N. B. (1984, March 20). *Federal efforts to improve America's teaching force* (Congressional Research Service, Library of Congress Publication No. 84-36S). Washington, DC: Congressional Research Service, Library of Congress.

Labaree, D. F. (1997). Public goods, private goods: The American struggle over educational goals. *American Educational Research Journal, 34*(1), 39-81.

Labaree, D. W. (1996). The trouble with ed schools. *Educational Foundations, 10*(1), 27-45.

Laitsch, D. (1998). The Massachusetts teacher tests: What happened? *AACTE Briefs, 19*(11), 1, 3.

Lucas, C. J. (1997). *Teacher education in America*. New York: St. Martin's.

Marshall, C. (1999). Research the margins: Feminist critical policy analysis. *Educational Policy, 13*(1), 59-76.

Mathews, J. (1999, April 20). A call for education change. *The Washington Post*, p. A3.

National Commission for Excellence in Teacher Education. (1985). *A call for change in teacher education*. Washington, DC: American Association of Colleges for Teacher Education.

National Commission on Teaching & America's Future. (1996). *What matters most: Teachers for America's future*. New York: Columbia University Press.

Phillips, J. R., & Kanstoroom, M. (1999). Title II: Does professional development work? In M. Kanstoroom & C. E. Finn, Jr. (Eds.), *New directions* (pp. 61-78). Washington, DC: Thomas B. Fordham Foundation.

Quality Teacher in Every Classroom Act, S. 1484, 105th Cong., 1st Sess. (1997).

Randall, E. V., Cooper, B. S., & Hite, S. J. (1999). Understanding the politics of research in education. *Educational Policy, 13*(1), 7-22.

Riley, R. W. (1999, February). *New challenges, a new resolve: Moving American education into the 21st century, the sixth annual state of American education speech*. Washington, DC: U.S. Department of Education.

Rotherham, A. (1999). *Toward performance-based federal education funding reauthorization of the Elementary and Secondary Education Act*. Washington, DC: Progressive Policy Institute, 21st Century Schools Project.

Sanchez, R. (1996, September 13). Teacher standards called "national shame." *The Washington Post*, pp. A1, A22.

Shaul, M. S. (1999, May 5). *Testimony presented to the Subcommittee on Postsecondary Education, Training, and Life-Long Learning*. Washington, DC: U.S. House of Representatives.

S. J. Res. 138 to establish a commission on teacher education. (1983, July 28).

Stedman, J. B. (1996, May 15). *Eisenhower professional development program: Moving beyond math and science* (Congressional Research Service, Library of Congress Publication No. 94-846 EPW). Washington, DC: Congressional Research Service, Library of Congress.

Stedman, J. B. (1998, December 3). *Teacher quality and quantity: Proposals in the 105th Congress* (Congressional Research Service, Library of Congress Publication No. 98-166 EPW). Washington, DC: Congressional Research Service, Library of Congress.

Stone, D. (1997). *Policy paradox: The art of political decision making*. New York: Norton.

Teacher Warranty Act of 1985, H.R. 937, 99th Cong., 1st Sess. (1985, February 4).

Thomas B. Fordham Foundation. (1999, April). *The teachers we need and how to get more of them* [Online]. Available: http://www.edexcellence.net

Whitmire, R. (1996, September 13). Report: Poorly trained teachers find their way into schools. *Courier-Journal*, pp. 1, 6.

Zoltan, D. (1997). Psychological processes in cooperative language learning: Group dynamics and motivation. *Modern Language Journal, 81*(4), 482-493.

The Role of Accreditation Reform in Teacher Education

FRANK B. MURRAY

There has been an undeniable erosion of the value and status of academic degrees in teacher education. The erosion has not been stemmed by traditional accreditation mechanisms that are based on mere consensus standard setting. It is argued that a new system of teacher education accreditation, based on evidence of student learning, valid assessment of student learning, and continuous program improvement based on evidence, is more likely to stem the erosion than the current approach.

A PROBLEM: THE EROSION OF THE TEACHER EDUCATION ACADEMIC DEGREE

Although the teacher education degree has rarely been held in high regard, there continues to be a steady and puzzling erosion of the value of academic degrees in teacher education and in the status of the colleges and schools that grant them (see Conant, 1963; Koerner, 1963; Judge, Lemosse, Paine, & Sedlak, 1994). It is puzzling because, since *A Nation at Risk* (National Commission on Excellence in Education, 1983), there have been sustained and concerted efforts to reform American teacher education (namely, the Holmes Group, the Project 30 Alliance, the Renaissance Group, the National Center for Educational Renewal, and the Teacher Education Initiative). These efforts were in addition to the ongoing work of the established teacher education organizations to improve teacher education programs (e.g., Association of Teacher Educators [ATE], Association of Colleges for Teacher Education [AACTE], and their state affiliates). Despite this prolonged effort, the members of the National Commission on Teaching & America's Future (NCTAF),

EDUCATIONAL POLICY, Vol. 14 No. 1, January and March 2000 40-59

many of whom also participated in the various teacher education reform movements, concluded in 1996 that the country was still not serious about standards for its teachers and that the nation's teacher education programs needed to be reinvented.

There are numerous examples of the lack of public and professional trust in the teacher education degree. Twenty-six states have added basic skills tests to the license requirements, a domain that ordinarily would be a presumed prerequisite to the college degree. Twenty-seven states retest the graduate's subject matter knowledge. The recent federal higher education reauthorization does not permit funds to go to an education school by itself, preferring instead that the education school partner with the more responsible public schools or arts and science colleges. So that the public can have assurances not provided by the education degree, Section 211 of Title II of the Higher Education Act requires that only education schools (not business, law, medical, physical therapy, or nursing schools) report the pass rate of its graduates on state licensing examinations. Less than half of the nation's education schools are accredited, a fact that has no appreciable consequence for a school's standing or the prospects for its graduates. The National Board for Professional Teaching Standards (NBPTS) elected not to require a degree in teacher education for its certification examinations. Alternative routes to the state's teaching license, increasingly popular with policy makers, invariably bypass the teacher education degree. Finally, the requirements for teaching licenses, even those based on graduation from a teacher education program, are easily waived, and the licenses are typically not required for private school teaching assignments. Aside from the occasional graduate's grateful testimony, it is rare to find tangible evidence that anyone, inside or outside the profession, has confidence in the education school degree or that it can be trusted to accomplish what the academic degree accomplishes in other fields.

THE CURRENT NATIONAL SYSTEM
OF TEACHER QUALITY

The NCTAF (1996), quite commendably and justifiably, seeks a competent, caring, and qualified teacher for each of the nation's 53 million elementary and secondary students, and it proposed a limited, but ambitious, set of actions to bring that about. In the commission's view, its goal will be met if the next generation of teachers meets a set of mutually reinforcing standards in three domains: (a) the state's teaching license, (b) the accreditation of the school of education, and (c) the certification of advanced teaching proficiency. For the most part, these standards are being developed by some members of the commission itself as part of its own long-standing effort to raise standards for the teaching profession.

Currently, there are about nine potential ingredients in the nation's fragmented and fragile system of quality assurance for teaching. Each one speaks, separately and indirectly, often weakly, to a different aspect of teacher quality. In seeking to determine whether a person, otherwise unknown to us, should be a teacher, we typically ask what the person studied, where the person studied it, how the person scored on standardized tests about some of it, what external agencies thought of the course of study and the place that offered it, what the hiring school thought of the person, what some professional societies and boards thought of the person's accomplishments and practices, and so forth.

Because no single ingredient indicates whether the person is caring, competent, and qualified, common sense and prudence require that we employ multiple, and independent, indicators of teaching quality and that they converge to show a consistent pattern about the person. The commission settled on three of these potential indicators—indicators derived from the state license, the accreditation of the teacher education institution, and, later, a national teaching certificate—to assure the public that the teacher is a competent, caring, and qualified person.

Two aspects of the commission's limited proposal may prove problematic, however. The first is that important corroborating, or disconfirming, information from the other indicators about teacher quality may be overlooked in the commission's three-pronged approach. Second—and more important—the critical requirement of measurement independence may be compromised if the standards and the agencies that undertake the evaluation of them are not independent of each other. This is a difficult problem to overcome when such a high value is also placed on systemic reform and consistency among the separate standards and agencies. However, in instances where the indicators and measures are known to be error laden, as is the case with all measures of teacher quality, it is axiomatic that the measures be independent of one another, thus reducing the contamination of documented measurement errors.

Nine interrelated ingredients in the current system of teacher quality assurance are presented below in the form of the question each answers about whether a person should be permitted to teach.

The academic degree. The question is, does the prospective teacher possess adequate knowledge of the liberal arts, the subject matters that will be taught, and pedagogical knowledge and its attendant skills and dispositions?

Actually, the question is more accurately put as, how well has the student conformed to the faculty's expectations in a course of study?

The program faculty's claim about any student's knowledge and skill is usually justified by the student's performance on about 100 hours of examinations over 4 to 5 years by about 40 separate evaluators (namely, the professors). The student may also have passed a prerequisite standardized test of academic potential or accomplishment, the SAT or ACT, both of which, by the way, are more demanding than any of the available standardized machine-scored tests of the teacher's basic skills competence. The grade-point index of these collective measures often meets fairly demanding psychometric criteria for stability and reliability, but evidence of its validity, which requires constant verification and documentation, is rarely provided. Without that documentation, we have no solid evidence that the student has mastered what the faculty have asserted or that it has any bearing on whether the student can teach well.

General and specialized accreditation. The question asked and answered by an accrediting agency (e.g., one of the regional accreditors and the National Council for Accreditation of Teacher Education [NCATE]) is, does the institution have the general and specific capacity to deliver the programs it intends to deliver? To some extent, classic accreditation is independent of whether the programs are delivered well; it is primarily a question about the capacity or ability of the institution, quite apart from its willingness to act on that capacity.

The question is traditionally answered in terms of a set of standards, which, if met, entitles the institution to be called a college, a university, or, in the specialized case, a school of education. Rarely, however, is there empirical evidence that the standards employed, attractive as they seem, truly matter with regard to the kind of education students actually experience.

License. The question is asked and answered by the state. It does not address the capacity or the diligence of an institution or really anything about the institution. The question is whether an individual candidate is minimally and legally acceptable, or qualified, as a teacher in the particular state. In many cases, the state avoids a direct answer to the question and grants the license automatically to graduates of programs it has approved. In some cases, it may grant the license if a state-prescribed set of academic courses is completed as part of a nonteacher education academic degree. Currently, the Interstate New Teachers Assessment and Support Consortium (INTASC) has formulated national standards for the license (statements of the knowledge, skill, and dispositions the beginning teacher should have independently of the standards currently embodied in accreditation and program approval).

Rather than go to the trouble of actually examining each candidate for a teaching license, as is often done for the driving license, for example, the states generally have posed a different, and less difficult, question for themselves. This question is, does the program, which the candidate completed, conform to certain standards established by an association of state directors of teacher certification? This is the question left unanswered in the typical accreditation evaluation, namely, what does the institution actually do with its capacity? But like the traditional accreditation evaluation, the worth of the standards, as right sounding as many seem, has not been empirically established.

Certificate. The question asked and answered by a standards board (e.g., NBPTS or a local equivalent) is, can the tenured teacher perform certain tasks that are presumed to indicate a higher level of teaching competence and understanding than that signified by the state license? The distinction between licenses and certificates is only recently made, the later being given, presumably, to master teachers, or at least very good teachers, in recognition of a kind of superior teaching competence and the teacher's articulate justification for it. At the present time, owing to their recent development, we do not have evidence of the validity of the assessments of these advanced standards.

Tenure. The question is asked and answered by a school district. The question is whether the hiring school district, based on its own assessment of 3 years or more of the teacher's work, wishes to retain the teacher's services for the duration of the teacher's career. Rarely, however, have school districts, or professional associations that partner in the controlling collective bargaining agreements, tested the validity of the means by which they grant tenure or permanent employment contracts.

Standardized tests. The question is asked and answered by an agency in collaboration with a test developer (e.g., Educational Testing Service). The question is whether the prospective teacher can respond correctly to a sufficient number of questions of interest to the agency to earn a passing score, typically in pedagogical and subject matter knowledge. The test, unlike almost every other form of teacher quality assessment, is subjected to several court-tested procedures for the validity and fairness of the passing score (the cut score). These court-tested procedures, however, are the lowest forms of validity and almost never rise to a level that would address the recommended validity categories (namely, content, concurrent, predictive, and construct) we find in undergraduate textbooks of educational evaluation and measurement.

Student achievement. Until recently, the question of student learning has rarely been asked, but the teacher's students answer it in a sense. The questions are, did the students profit from the teacher's efforts, and did they acquire information, knowledge, skill, and dispositions they did not have prior to the instructional program? The answer is the student's achievement gain, which is presumed to have a systematic relationship with teaching but may not if other factors, particularly nonschool factors, play greater roles in the student's achievement than the teacher's work (Ferguson, 1991).

Merit awards and prizes. The question is, has the teacher taught in an exemplary and satisfactory manner? It is typically answered by the school district and state with merit salary awards. It is answered in other cases by panels of experts who award prizes and honors for teaching excellence (such as teacher of the year awards). The validity of these determinations, like the validity of many of the other ingredients in the national system, has not been determined.

The public's view of teaching. As above, the question is, has the teacher taught in an exemplary and satisfactory manner? The public's answer or view of exemplary teaching can be considered as a ninth factor, equally unvalidated but no less influential, given the practice of governance of the schools by lay boards and legislators. It holds that exemplary teaching entails telling the truth publicly in an engaging manner, assessing students' learning of the told material, and maintaining classroom order and decorum. The public view largely rules out the tenets of progressive education or the current school reform notions of "all kids can learn," "less is more," "authentic assessment," and the family of practices and attitudes embedded in a constructivist view of pedagogical practice. It also rules out counterintuitive research findings on social promotion, mixed ability grouping, and cooperative learning, for example.

Although none of the answers to these questions, nor the ingredients by themselves, conclusively determines whether the teacher can in fact teach well, these ingredients, taken together, provide convergent evidence on the subject. Any one by itself is subject to known distortions that may suggest that a person can teach well, or at an acceptable level, when in fact the person will prove to be inept with some pupils in some circumstances.

In matters of importance, where mistakes have significant costs, prudent societies institute systems of checks and balances supported by multiple measures. Even in biological systems, vital functions are overdetermined through multiple failsafe mechanisms (birds, for example, have several independent navigational systems on which to draw; similarly, humans have multiple modes of communication should any single mode fail).

PROPOSED SOLUTIONS: STANDARDS
VERSUS EVIDENCE FOR CLAIMS

The NCTAF has proposed a Flexner strategy to remedy the problems associated with the decline of teacher education and the alleged low performance of America's teachers (see Berliner & Biddle, 1996, for the case that American teaching has not failed to the extent claimed in the reform reports). It is a three-pronged effort to raise standards for the (a) teaching license, (b) accreditation of education schools, and (c) performance of tenured teachers. This proposal, admirable in so many respects, unfortunately requires a professional knowledge base that is more settled than the one we actually have (see Murray, 1996, for an account of the overall tentative nature of the knowledge base for teacher education, despite solid advances in some domains).

It requires, as well, standards based on this emerging knowledge base. The knowledge base we have is also less steady and certain than would be needed to justify the proposed political imposition of these standards. Perhaps this is the reason the Council for Basic Education, the Fordham Foundation, and the American Federation of Teachers (AFT) have not found consistency in the curriculum standards of the various states (see Archbald, 1998, for an account of these discrepancies). Along the same lines, the validation of the INTASC, NCATE, and NBPTS standards is only now beginning as part of the National Partnership for Excellence and Accountability in Teaching Office of Educational Research and Improvement contract.

Owing to the emerging nature of the knowledge base, there are few settled policies in the field of education, even on such general administrative questions as social promotion, tracking, grouping, skipping grades, early entrance, year-round schooling, family groupings, nongraded schooling, optimal class size, school uniforms, corporal punishment, and so forth. There is less agreement on more fundamental educational issues: the nonnegotiable core curriculum, the role of memorization, the dependability of specific and nonspecific transfer, the utility of bilingual instruction, portfolio assessment, the role of IQ tests in the school, and so forth. The subject matter areas are equally unsettled. Should initial reading instruction be whole word or language, phonics based; should elementary pupils have calculators in their math classes; should they memorize the algorithms and tables; is social studies really history; and is creationism a legitimate component of the science curriculum?

This is not to deny the mass of educational research on these questions, much of it unfortunately below common research standards (Howe, 1982). A growing and significant portion of the mass is sound but often conflicting in its implications for practice. The fact is that the standing of educational research is not much better than the standing of education schools, not surprising as the faculty of education schools do most of the research in the field. The point is that despite an improving research base in education, many matters are unsettled, and there is little professional agreement on the practices that should be adopted. To the extent there is agreement, it is on what should not be done rather than what should be done.

Apart from the low standing of the knowledge base for educational practice, a weakness in the NCTAF proposal is that the standards on which its recommendations are based (namely, INTASC, NCATE, and NBPTS) are all under development and have not been validated; they are provisional, untested, and built only on a consensus of well-intentioned professional educators. It is entirely possible that owing to the unproven nature of these current consensus standards, an education school could meet them and we, and more important it, would still not know whether the candidates for the degree had mastered critical knowledge and skill, whether the faculty's assessment system was valid, and whether the faculty based its decisions on a functioning quality control system that could locate weaknesses in the program.

The development of an alternative solution to remedy these weaknesses has been proposed by the Teacher Education Accreditation Council (TEAC) (1999). This proposal addresses the quality control system the teacher education faculty has in place and the evidence that the system yields about the health and accomplishments of the teacher education degree programs. More important, it requires that there be solid and convincing evidence about the one element that is currently in doubt about today's teacher education programs— have the graduates in fact acquired the knowledge, disposition, and skill their academic degree indicates? The approach advocated by this new council is also applicable to each of the other elements in the nation's quality assurance system— namely, each of these elements should base its determinations and assertions on evidence, not merely its own consensus about how things ought to be.

ISSUES IN THE NEW APPROACH TO
TEACHER EDUCATION ACCREDITATION

A Different Question

Typically, accreditation is an assessment of the institution's capacity to be a college or university—whether it, in other words, deserves to be called a college or university. In the case of specialized accreditation, the question is whether the unit deserves to be called a college or school of education. The TEAC is primarily concerned with another issue: what the institution does with that capacity in teacher education and whether it has solid, credible evidence to back up its claims for what it does. The TEAC, in other words, seeks to answer different questions about the institution, questions every institution should ask of itself; namely, is there a credible reason to believe it has actually accomplished what it thinks it has accomplished, how does it know, and is the evidence strong enough to convince disinterested experts?

An Unproven System

The notion of accreditation by the audit of the evidence of quality has only recently appeared in the professional literature here and abroad (Dill, Massy, Williams, & Cook, 1996; Graham, Lyman, & Trow, 1995; Trow, 1998). The TEAC is currently testing the concept in a pilot study, supported by the Fund to Improve Post Secondary Education and the Pew Charitable Trusts, and it is possible that the concept may be too difficult for some institutions to implement successfully at this time. But it should not be out of the reach of those who have based their work on evidence.

Educational reform generally proceeds in exactly the way the TEAC is proceeding. The NBPTS, armed with little more than the idea that the standards for certification should be separated from the standards for licensure, launched a new organization on the promise that credible standards for certification could be developed and reliably assessed. The jury is still out on whether it succeeded, but few would deny that its work to date has advanced the profession.

Dominance of the Unaccredited

There is probably no single reason why the majority of education schools is not accredited. Some institutions undoubtedly feel they could not meet the current NCATE standards, the only standards that have been available for the accreditation of teacher education units. Others feel these standards are irrelevant, unproven, or wrongheaded. Some institutions believe the effort to comply with these standards would actually weaken their programs, and others seemingly cannot be bothered because currently accreditation in teacher education confers few tangible benefits on the institution. Whatever the reasons, it is not in the profession's or the nation's interest to have so many institutions bypass accreditation, particularly so many of the nation's leading institutions.

Two Accrediting Agencies

Rarely has America thought a monopoly was the better way to organize society—whether it be education, religion, public safety, the judiciary, commerce, the press, transportation, or communications. We have generally held to the idea that multiple views, approaches, and solutions serve us best. Only as a last resort have we adopted standardization and uniformity in truly important matters. When we do, we also put in place systems of checks and balances so that those granted monopolies are limited in their influence.

The cause of teacher unionism has probably not been held back, for example, by the fact that there are two unions, the National Education Association (NEA) and the AFT. Why should the cause of accreditation be weakened by the fact of two accrediting agencies? The professions of law and business (and shortly, nursing) also seem not to have been held back by the existence of multiple accrediting agencies.

The cause of higher education has not been held back by the fact that there are 3,000 or so colleges and universities, each with its own distinctive standard, mission, and point of view. Nor has the cause of schooling been held back by the fact that there are 15,000 school districts and scores of private schools, each with its own standards and approach.

It did not have to be this way; we could have had one standardized approach in each area, but when the opportunities presented themselves historically, the nation invariably chose diversity and a pluralistic approach to high-stakes matters.

Value in a Dual Approach

Fifty years ago, when massive numbers of new students sought higher education, college admissions officers were faced with evaluating students who had graduated from high schools that were of unknown quality. The officers attempted to solve their problem by putting in place a common examination for all students, regardless of their high school's reputation.

Some felt the examination should be about the student's aptitude for college work, whereas others felt the student's aptitude or capacity for college work missed the point or gave an unearned advantage to some groups of students. These others felt the student's academic accomplishment was the better and fairer measure, and the examination should be about what the student had learned in high school. Thus, we had two distinct theories about what might have been a simple and straightforward question: how to predict success in college.

Both approaches, the SAT and the ACT, worked equally well in the end despite their founding differences. Both were also important to the country when national admission scores precipitously declined because the decline occurred on both tests. Had only one shown a decline, the country might have had a different view about how much the nation was at risk. Thus, the country is often well served by different approaches to the same end.

The country wants to know whether its teacher education programs deliver what they claim to deliver in their mission statements—competent, well-educated teachers. One can attempt to answer the question indirectly through an investigation of whether the program conforms to a set of standards, established by the consensus of representatives of key segments of the profession, or one can directly examine the evidence for the claims about quality. The TEAC has chosen the latter approach.

These are not mutually exclusive approaches any more than the SAT and the ACT are mutually exclusive. The results of each will inform the other. They are different approaches based on differing analyses about what serves the institution, the profession, and the public best.

Legitimacy of Accreditation

Generally, it is thought that accreditors derive their legitimacy from the fact that they represent the field. No organization, however, has successfully found a way to capture the full diversity in American education. Who, in fact, is authorized to speak for all teachers (not just those affiliated with the NEA or AFT), all administrators, school boards, professors, and so on? More to the point, the field also includes the faculties in the arts and sciences, whose disciplines are being taught in the schools, and these groups have not been historically represented as part of the national accreditation movements in teacher education.

The legitimacy issue, when cast as a sampling problem of the field's components, remains unsolved because the field has not found a way to legitimize any person or groups of persons as spokespersons or representatives of the entire field. Legitimacy, rather than a "who is entitled to speak for us" issue, can be recast as an issue of the "evidence that speaks for itself." In this case, it may not be as important to interrogate the legitimacy of those who speak about the quality of education schools, since their legitimacy will be derived from the quality of their evidence.

What kind of evidence would speak for itself? Evidence that the graduates of a Tennessee education school, for example, were overrepresented in the category of teachers whose students consistently made large academic gains in the Tennessee study of student achievement gains and underrepresented in the category of teachers whose students suffered small academic gains (Sanders & Rivers, 1996; Wright, Horn, & Sanders, 1997) would trump evidence that the school did, or did not, meet any of the commonly articulated standards about the education school's curriculum and administrative organization.

The Role of Standards

The problems of American education do not reside in the articulation of standards as much as they reside in the evidence we have about whether we have met the standards. There is, in fact, very little substantive difference in the written standards for teacher education advocated by the major reform groups. The writing and pronouncement of standards, although time consuming and tendentious, turn out to be the easier, less expensive part of a reform. The harder part is finding solid evidence that indicates that standards have been met, exceeded, or failed.

What matters most is that the standards be genuine, thought through by the institution, make sense within the institution, be provisional and subject to revision as better data become available, and be the institution's, not someone else's, standards. Not any standards will do, in other words, but only proven standards that can be shown to solve problems the institution seeks to solve. Standards that lead to a rise in academic achievement in the schools and can be shown to lead to more caring, competent, and qualified teachers are the only standards that should matter.

There are two aspects of standards, each somewhat in conflict with the other. Standard, as in the flag of the rallying point, denotes a call to higher achievement, higher purpose, and greater effort. Standard in the other sense denotes conformity, lack of variation, inflexibility—as in standardization. At the moment, most professional educational standards are formulated at fairly abstract levels so it has not been possible to really test and prove them. Others are quite specific and prescriptive, for example, about how teacher education should be administered and organized. These also have not been tested empirically, and their opposites might work just as well.

Many others standards are clearer in the negative than in the positive, so we know more about what they are not than about what they are. "All children can learn" is an admirable standard and sentiment for teacher education programs. It is taken to mean that tracking and ability grouping should be avoided. It is less clear which positive programs should be put in their place in the education of special education or gifted students, however. The field, in other words, still has much work to do before it knows the full meaning and worth of many of the reform slogans and standards it has so enthusiastically adopted in the current standards-based reform movements.

More to the point, the current standards, on close reading, give teacher educators little guidance on key questions—such as the relative roles of phonics and calculators in reading and mathematics instruction, for example. The teaching profession does not have, despite the pronouncement of standards, a clear conception of educational malpractice. Until it does, the noble standards it enacts are somewhat premature. They certainly await confirmation by further research.

For this reason, accreditation based solely on an institution's conformity to standards, set largely by a well-meaning political consensus, has its own risks. We simply do not have the evidence for many standards at this time. Few standardized educational practices and innovations are grounded in solid research, and yet so many of them have had the support of the profession. If only because some have proven demonstrably harmful to students and their teachers, we should be cautious about standards that are based on little more than the consensus of large segments of the profession. It was standard practice, to take two recent egregious examples, to switch left-handed students to right-handed performance or beat pupils who failed the school's standards for deportment or academic accomplishment. In teacher education, it was a standard, and an equally wrongheaded and harmful practice, to exclude overweight and unattractive students from teacher education programs on the grounds they would not be effective with, or accepted by, their pupils.

The Relationship Between Accreditation Standards

The NCATE and the National Association of State Directors of Teacher Education Certification (NASDTEC) standards are compatible and consistent with TEAC standards for the evidence of student learning, validity of the assessment system, and functioning of the quality control system. The TEAC accreditation process would simply evaluate and audit the program faculty's evidence that they have met the NCATE or NASDTEC standards—or any other set of standards, based on the scholarly literature, that has as its goal the preparation of competent, caring, and qualified teachers.

Some states have required recently that the state program approval process be based on NCATE rather than the traditional NASDTEC standards. This requirement is not, in and of itself, an obstacle to accreditation by a system that audits evidence that standards adopted by an institution have been met.

Other Advantages of the New System

There are other very important and fundamental reasons that commend the new system of accreditation. It is possible, for example, to have students accept and conform to standards set by teachers and others. It is almost impossible to have that practice lead to genuine understanding and higher levels of mental functioning. The practice leads rather to concepts that are learned but not understood, that are short lived and deprived of the flexibility that characterizes knowledge. Modern views of intelligence and cognition, let along pedagogy, are clear that understanding and knowing are negotiated, situated, and constructed—all features of our minds that resist externally produced aims and purposes. The attainment of high standards is based, ironically, less on efforts to conform to them than on more indirect, ambitious, and subtle means that are in the rigorous service of the student's own problems and aspirations. Unlike information, knowledge cannot be simply given to the student; to require that it be memorized or imitated corrupts and limits its power.

Colleges, like individuals, also develop and mature. The key to understanding where a college might be in its development is to understand the evidence and reasons the college advances for its activities. The reclaiming of the American trust in higher education, and in teacher education, requires the academic community to have very thoughtful and principled reasons for its actions and decisions. As in the assessment of moral development, it is the nature of the reason, more than the action itself, that determines whether a practice is at, above, or below a standard or stage.

Compatibility With the New System

Some teacher education programs are driven by a set of ongoing organizational needs that put nearly all the available faculty and administration time and energy in the service of building an enduring fiscal and administrative structure for the program. The reasons they have for what they do are invariably tied to these overwhelming survival issues. Other programs, having built a sound structure for their work, turn their attention, resources, and energy to the task of establishing a position for the program within the college or university and local community. Others, when their local place and reputation are secured, are often motivated to have their work recognized and accepted by the national higher education and professional community. The program's allocation of resources and other actions, often puzzling from the perspectives of an earlier goal, now make sense as an effort to earn the "national visibility" that characterizes departments and colleges that seek national recognition and validation.

Some programs are less sensitive to the consequences of their actions for organizational traditions or their local and national reputations. These programs seem able to work through their convictions and act on them without undue regard for how other colleges and universities are conducting their affairs. Nearly everything in these programs depends on the quality of the evidence and reasons the program advances for taking an action, even though the action might be the very one that was taken earlier to acquire fiscal stability, a local or a national position. These programs should find the new approach highly congenial.

A program faculty, to take a simple example, might require SAT or ACT scores for admission. They might do this because it would simplify the admission decision, or because a dean uses the scores as a device for awarding scholarships and other support funds, or because the program saw its national reputation in terms of the selectively high scores of their students. However, the program faculty might have thought through their admission's practice in terms of the predictive or construct validity of the test and based their decision on the evidence of validity for their program.

Attempts to increase minority participation in the teacher education program, to take a more sensitive example, could be done simply to attract new markets; to conform to the requirements of some agency or board; to be in line with the prevailing views of some national foundations and important professional organizations; or because the pursuit of truth, the program's central concern, would be enhanced by bringing multiple perspectives to bear on every important educational question. Or, the program faculty might have done it because they thought, based on a political or moral philosophy, that it was simply the right thing to do.

Historically, schools that thought matters through for themselves and arrived at novel and productive solutions to the advancement of teaching and knowledge are credited with the important developments in higher education. These schools and programs would find the TEAC's audit approach to accreditation highly congenial and supportive.

The Success of the New System of Accreditation

It is too easy to say that the new system will have succeeded when all teacher education institutions are accredited—although that would be part of the story. It is too glib, and wrong, to say when the NCATE is replaced, because the NCATE is an important and an essential element in making teaching a true profession. The TEAC's competition is not the NCATE, nor is its work battling it for a share of the accreditation market. The TEAC's competition, in a sense, is the same as the NCATE's; it is all the unaccredited teacher education institutions, including those who have rejected the NCATE's methods. The TEAC is battling to create a market—getting institutions to see how much accreditation by audit will assist them and the profession.

It is perhaps unrealistic, although correct, to say that the TEAC will have succeeded when the public has confidence in its educators and values the means by which they were educated. One near-term sign of success might be that institutions would view their institutional accreditation report as they view their other scholarly work—something in which they would take pride, something they would see as a contribution to the field because it made a convincing case, something that would advance our knowledge about what works and what does not, something that would be broadly published and debated, and something that would stimulate the next round of experimentation and success.

We need to see faculty in education and in the arts and sciences turn the tools of their scholarship on themselves. Teacher educators should hold the same standards for their programs as they hold for their scholarship. Regrettably, we have not seen that across the board; we need to put in place a system that encourages people to do precisely that.

A STRATEGY TO STEM THE EROSION
OF THE TEACHER EDUCATION DEGREE

Ironically, teaching looks like a profession: It has professional degrees, licenses, certificates, national examinations, accreditation, state program approval, tenure reviews, recertification, professional development requirements, professional associations, and so forth. Few within or outside the profession have much confidence in any of the above. Many, for example, would willingly waive or terminate any of the above in response to teacher shortages. Others even seek to waive or terminate them as reform measures in themselves.

A large part of the problem is that the profession has not grounded its work in scholarly evidence. The TEAC's system centers on the academic degree program and the system the institution has in place to satisfy itself and others that its claims about itself and its students are warranted and can withstand scrutiny. This evidence is only one piece of the puzzle, however—a piece that speaks only to whether the students learned what program faculty taught them about critical professional knowledge, disposition, and skill.

Even if the new system succeeds, we know that the evidence institutions would have for their claims, although sound and a marked advance over typical practice, is likely to be inconclusive about whether a particular degree holder should teach. The public's confidence in the quality of its professional educators must rest on multiple and converging lines of evidence about the quality of the individuals who wish to teach. The new system provides only one of these several lines of evidence, namely, an audit of the quality of the evidence the institution uses in the award of the professional degree.

The other lines of evidence must come from independent assessments by others of different aspects of the prospective educator's competence. The states must secure independent evidence to warrant the granting of a license, school boards must secure their own evidence with regard to the hiring and tenure decisions, standards boards must secure their own evidence to justify the granting of certificates, professional societies must devise their own kinds of evidence for the award of prizes and trophies, and so forth. Because all the known measures and sources of evidence are subject to documented distortions and flaws, it is critical that the public have independent lines of evidence on the various aspects of educators' competencies: whether they have studied and mastered what matters, whether they are entitled to a license, whether they should be hired and tenured, whether they deserve merit payments, promotions, awards, and so forth.

The key point is that there be solid evidence, grounded in the professional literature, to warrant the granting of degrees, licenses, certificates, professional positions, tenure, merit payments, promotions, and awards. The TEAC's reform initiative, although purposefully limited to the audit of evidence about the academic degree, applies with equal force to the work of all other constituents of the profession.

The prerequisite to the rise of the public's confidence in its professional educators is the audit of the quality control systems the other parties of the profession have in place for the decisions entrusted to them by the public. When these independent lines of evidence converge and agree with each other, the public will have confidence that we have the right person in the school. At that time, its confidence will also be justified.

In April 1998, the fact that 59% of the candidates for the Massachusetts teacher license failed the state's new examination, many of them graduates of accredited schools of education, further eroded the public's confidence in education schools and alarmed policy makers nationwide. The fact that the test violated nearly every psychometric principle went unnoticed. Although it was regrettable that so many failed the flawed test, what was more regrettable was that no one brought forth better evidence that the degree holders were competent beginning teachers. This is precisely the kind of evidence TEAC-accredited programs would have available to refute claims based on unworthy tests.

A FINAL WORD ABOUT POLITICS
IN EDUCATION

One might have thought that the members of the NCTAF, and other reform-minded teacher educators, would have seen the invention of the TEAC as a welcome partner in the NCTAF goal that all education schools be accredited. After all, with more than half the education schools avoiding accreditation, despite having 45 years in which to obtain it, a new system that encouraged the unaccredited to obtain solid empirical evidence of their accomplishments might be seen, on the face of it, as supporting the NCTAF agenda.

That, however, has not been the response the TEAC has had (see Basinger, 1998, for an account of the TEAC's hostile reception by some segments of the teacher education community). The fact that this new system is so single-mindedly and passionately opposed, often by those who have had no opportunity to understand it, is an indicator that more is at issue than a better way to accredit education schools. It is an indicator of the unseemly side of the politics of education in which the merits of alternative systems are subservient to a political agenda.

It is possible that some could be concerned that the TEAC would lower quality, that some schools that could not meet NCATE standards could satisfy TEAC standards.[1] What is odd about this particular concern is that the TEAC has grounded its accreditation decision not in an institution's conformity to unproven consensus standards but in solid evidence that the teacher education program's students have learned what was expected of them, that the system of measuring that learning was valid, and that there is convincing evidence that the program has a sound quality control system in place that addresses all aspects of the evidence for the quality of the program. What, in other words, could be the problem with accreditation-based evidence that the program that already conforms to state standards has in fact accomplished what it claims it has accomplished?

It might be that there is no problem with this aspect of the TEAC's proposal; that is, institutions and the public would each profit from the new approach. It is simply, on the face of it, a good thing to do. The problem is that it should not be confused with accreditation; that is, the "A" in TEAC more accurately refers to the audit, or accountability, or assistance, but not accreditation.

For the time being, this must remain an open question because the basis and purpose of accreditation is shifting (see Dill et al., 1996; Graham et al., 1995; Trow, 1998). At one time, it was merely a device for colleges to determine from which other institutions they should accept transfer students.

Later, it became the basis by which the federal government could determine who should receive federal funds for students and some other purposes. Specialized accreditation is now proposed as the basis on which states would grant a teaching license and districts would hire. Accreditation, in other words, is an evolving construct that might very well accommodate the new system that the TEAC and others have proposed.

What is most in doubt in the minds of policy makers and the public, however, is the value of professional teacher education. They simply doubt it accomplishes anything of value and worry that it in fact undermines the value that would otherwise have been obtained had teachers been selected from those who were not enrolled in teacher education programs. The public is not concerned that standards compiled by teacher educators, teacher unions, school administrators, and the many specialized professional educator groups are not adhered to. In the public's mind, these professionally self-serving standards are the problem, not the solution to the problem. What everyone wants to see is some credible evidence that tomorrow's teachers can teach at the high levels expected of them. A system of accreditation that is not about this evidence will not help stem the erosion of the teacher education degree.

NOTE

1. It is entirely possible, as some have claimed, that the TEAC's system is far more demanding and difficult than the NCATE's system because the standards of evidence are higher. This may be one reason why the NCATE is moving toward a TEAC system in the NCATE 2000 redesign in which performance-based evidence of student learning is required.

REFERENCES

Archbald, D. (1998). *The reviews of state content standards in English language arts and mathematics: A summary and review of their methods and findings and implications for future standards development.* Unpublished report for the National Education Goals Panel.

Basinger, J. (1998, October 9). Fight intensifies over accreditation of teacher-education programs. *Chronicle of Higher Education*, pp. A12-A13.

Berliner, D., & Biddle, D. (1996). *The manufactured crisis.* New York: Addison-Wesley.

Conant, J. B. (1963). *Education of American teachers.* New York: McGraw-Hill.

Dill, D., Massy, W., Williams, P., & Cook, C. (1996, September and October). Accreditation & academic quality assurance: Can we get there from here? *Change Magazine*, pp. 17-24.

Ferguson, R. (1991). Paying for public education: New evidence of how and why money matters. *Harvard Journal on Legislation, 28*, 465-498.

Graham, P., Lyman, R., & Trow, M. (1995). *Accountability of colleges and universities: An essay.* New York: Columbia University Press.

Howe, H. (1982). Forward. In H. Judge (Ed.), *American graduate schools of education: A view from abroad.* New York: Ford Foundation.

Judge, H., Lemosse, M., Paine, M., & Sedlak, M. (1994). The university and the teachers. *Oxford Studies in Comparative Education, 4*(1-2).

Koerner, J. D. (1963). *The miseducation of American teachers*. Boston: Houghton Mifflin.

Murray, F. (Ed.). (1996). *The teacher educator's handbook: Building a knowledge base for the preparation of teachers*. San Francisco: Jossey-Bass.

National Commission on Excellence in Education. (1983). *A nation at risk*. Washington, DC: Government Printing Office.

National Commission on Teaching & America's Future. (1996). *What matters most: Teaching for America's future*. New York: Author.

Sanders, W., & Rivers, J. (1996). *Cumulative and residual effects of teachers on future student academic achievement*. Knoxville: University of Tennessee Value-Added Research and Development Center.

Teacher Education Accreditation Council. (1999). *Prospectus*. Washington, DC: Author.

Trow, M. (1998). On the accountability of higher education in the United States. In W. Bowen & H. Shapiro (Eds.), *Universities and their leadership* (pp. 15-61). Princeton, NJ: Princeton University Press.

Wright, S., Horn, S., & Sanders, W. (1997). Teacher and classroom context effects on student achievement: Implications for teacher evaluation. *Journal of Personnel Evaluation in Education*, 57-67.

Part 2

Stories From the State Arena

Autonomous Boards and Standards-Based Teacher Development

MARILYN M. SCANNELL
and PHILIP L. METCALF

This article provides a history of the Indiana Professional Standards Board in governing teacher preparation and licensure and the redesign of the state's teacher preparation and licensure system. The authors conclude that although there are tremendous challenges ahead, the board has earned the respect of education constituencies within the state and has been an effective force in bringing these constituencies to the table to discuss the issues facing teacher quality in Indiana.

IN THIS ARTICLE, we provide a history of the Indiana Professional Standards Board (IPSB) in governing teacher preparation and licensure and the redesign of the state's teacher preparation and licensure system. We discuss the formation of the board, its redesign process and policies and their implications, its achievements to date, and the challenges it still faces. We believe that Indiana's experiences to date will be instructive to other states aspiring to move to a standards-based teacher preparation and licensing system. We wish we had all of the answers but must instead caution the reader that, although the IPSB has accomplished a great deal during its 7-year history, much work remains to be done if the board's vision is to become a reality.

ESTABLISHING THE BOARD—THE TIME WAS RIGHT

During the recent legislative session, when the IPSB's budget request was not granted, a colleague pointed out that we often think we are writing the

EDUCATIONAL POLICY, Vol. 14 No. 1, January and March 2000 61-76
© 2000 Corwin Press, Inc.

book when instead we are writing a chapter in the book. Indeed, there are many chapters in the IPSB's history, which began with the 1989 legislative session when a bill was introduced to create a professional standards board. Instead of creating the board, however, legislators created a 15-member study commission. The commission was directed to (a) evaluate Indiana's existing system for teacher licensing and certification, (b) evaluate teacher preparation programs, (c) recommend improvements for (a) and (b), (d) provide the fiscal impact of any recommendations made, and (e) study and make recommendations on any other matter related to teacher certification and licensing.

After gathering research and hearing testimony from individuals and associations, the commission recommended the establishment of an autonomous professional standards board, which would exercise final regulatory authority over educational licensing and accreditation processes. This recommendation was not unanimous; however, it was supported by the majority of members composed of teachers and higher education representatives. Over the next several years, legislation to create a standards board was introduced annually; however, it was not until 1992 that the "right" conditions existed for legislation to pass. These conditions included the existence of strong teachers' associations able to persuade legislators of the value of a standards board and a Democratic governor willing to sign the bill into law. Thus, the autonomous IPSB was created by Public Law 46-1992.

BOARD COMPOSITION AND POWERS

The board created by this legislation was intended to represent all components of the education profession. It consisted of 16 members, 15 of whom were appointed by the governor for 4-year terms, and the state superintendent of public instruction, who serves as an ex-officio member. Eleven of the appointed members were required to hold valid Indiana teacher's licenses and be actively employed by a school corporation. These members represent specific subjects, positions, and grade levels including a district superintendent; a principal; early childhood, elementary, middle/junior high, special education, vocational education, English/language arts, mathematics, and science teachers; a student services representative; three members representing Indiana teacher preparation units within public and private higher education institutions who must hold a teacher's license (not necessarily from Indiana) and be actively employed by the respective teacher preparation unit; and a school board member. A few years later, legislation was introduced to create a separate standards board for administrators, supported by associations of superintendents, school boards, and principals. However, a compromise was reached, and three new members were added to the board. The new members, a special education director, an additional principal, and a business representative, brought the board's total membership to 19.

The board's powers are broad. As outlined in the legislation, they include

governing teacher training and licensing programs. Notwithstanding any other law, the board and the board's staff have the sole authority and responsibility for making recommendations concerning and otherwise governing teacher training and teacher licensing matters. (Indiana Code, Title 20, 1998, p. 19)

Included in the legislation's definition of teachers were administrators and student services personnel.

The staff and the funds that previously supported teacher training and licensing functions within the Indiana Department of Education were transferred to the newly created autonomous board. One of the staff, who had overseen these functions within the department, was appointed by the governor to serve as the executive director. Thus, the board was fortunate to have from its inception some funds with which to work and a dedicated and knowledgeable staff who could continue the day-to-day responsibilities and functions assigned to the board while it worked to establish itself as an independent agency and provide leadership to the education profession.

Of significance was the fact that all functions related to teacher preparation and licensing and all education personnel requiring licenses were within the board's purview, allowing future board policies to be comprehensive in nature. Also significant are the board's dual roles, that of a professional board responsible for determining policies for professional preparation and licensing and a state agency responsible for issuing licenses and monitoring the accreditation process for teacher preparation programs, teacher testing, the beginning teacher internship program, and continuing education (relicensure) requirements. These dual roles eventually led to a restructuring of the agency to enable staff to more effectively contribute to the board's development of and transition to a new preparation and licensing system while efficiently meeting ongoing agency responsibilities.

DETERMINING THE BOARD'S
PROCESS, MISSION, AND VISION

The board elected a dean of education from a large public institution as its first chair and classroom teachers as vice chair and secretary/parliamentarian. In 1994, the chair was succeeded by a classroom teacher who led the board for the next 5 years. At that time, the board also elected a principal as vice chair and reelected the teacher who served as secretary/parliamentarian, both of whom also continued in their positions for the next 5 years. Thus, the board is fortunate to have had stable leadership to guide it through its initial development and continued growth throughout its 7-year existence.

In its early days, the board struggled with its identity. For most board members, serving on a board representing the state in a public forum governed by open-door laws, rather than representing a specific constituency, was a new experience. It is a tribute to the board that its members were able to rise above special interests and focus instead on what was best for the teaching profession and for children in Indiana classrooms. Board members take great pride in the fact that observers at their meetings are unable to connect individual board members with specific interest groups. To ensure that the board's focus remains on the "big picture," a board member code of ethics was created and is monitored by one of the board's committees.

Opposition to the board continued during its first 2 years of existence, stemming primarily from the administrators' and school boards' associations that were concerned that the teachers' associations would control board decisions for their own political gain. The state superintendent of public instruction who originally served on the board made clear his opposition to the board's creation and stated he would do everything in his power to put it out of business. However, the board and its leadership demonstrated through an open and deliberate course of action the ability to positively influence the direction of teacher preparation and licensure in the state and to reach out to all stakeholder groups in the process.

At its second meeting, the board recognized that if it were to be a positive instrument for the education profession, it must develop a vision and beliefs that would guide its future decisions. To accomplish this task, the board met an extra day each month, made possible by a grant from the Lilly Endowment, Inc. During this time, the board read numerous articles, received testimony from education experts across the United States and within Indiana, and conducted its regular business in fulfillment of its regulatory responsibilities.

After extensive preparation, the board developed vision and mission statements, adopted unanimously at its 1993 summer retreat. The board's mission, which is "to establish and maintain rigorous, achievable standards for educators beginning with preservice preparation and continuing throughout their professional careers," has served as the basis for the board's ensuing work. To fulfill its new mission, the board decided that a review of the existing rules for teacher preparation and licensure, which had not been reviewed for 19 years, was necessary. The original plan for conducting this review called for all rules revision to be completed within 1 year. It soon became evident, however, that the task was much more extensive than originally planned and that a systemic reform required more than rules revision.

THE DECISION TO MOVE TO A STANDARDS-BASED PREPARATION AND LICENSING SYSTEM

Several events took place in 1994 that influenced the direction of the board's work. The original executive director decided to retire, and a new executive director was hired. The board's recommendation to the governor for the position was an individual who had extensive national experience as a staff member with the American Association of Colleges for Teacher Education. As a result of the firm foundation established by the board and its leadership during the first 2 years, the board was ready to move its agenda forward at a faster pace. A committee structure, including an executive committee, was established to govern the board's work. It is significant that several of the board members, including both of the board chairs, had national connections with such organizations as the American Association of Colleges for Teacher Education, the National Education Association, the National Board for Professional Teaching Standards (NBPTS), and the National Council for Accreditation of Teacher Education (NCATE). Unlike many other states that avoided connections with national groups, the IPSB sought to build on these connections.

In-state connections and working relationships were equally important to board members. By this time, they had developed a comfortable working relationship with a district superintendent, who had formerly employed one of the board members, and had previously worked with the board as a facilitator to develop its mission and vision. At its July 19-20, 1994, retreat, he led the board through a process that would determine its future for the next decade and beyond. The first step in the process called for the board to examine its current system, Rules 46 and 47, in which licensing is based on completion of a teacher preparation program, consisting of state-prescribed course work and credit hours and passing certain testing requirements. Twenty-four strengths of the current system were identified and compared to 33 limitations. Primary strengths included the ease with which the course and credit hour approach could be implemented and its compatibility with other states. Primary limitations included the system's focus on inputs rather than outcomes, teaching of the subject rather than the student, and its lack of connections with the state's curriculum goals for K-12 students. The board then reviewed the components of a performance-based system for preparing and licensing teachers and identified 32 strengths associated with this system as compared to 24 limitations. Strengths included its alignment with state-of-the-art educational reform initiatives under way through the Interstate New Teacher Assessment and Support Consortium (INTASC), the NCATE, and the NBPTS and its focus on learners rather than courses. Concerns included cost, the need for complex assessment instruments, and the fact that it was not yet supported by empirical evidence demonstrating that the new system would produce better results.

Despite these concerns, however, the board took decisive steps at this retreat toward the implementation of a new performance-based system, including the following:

- Adopt the 10 core principles for licensing beginning teachers developed by the INTASC (1992)
- Form advisory groups to develop performance-based standards for specific licensing areas, which build on the 10 core INTASC principles.

Two initial advisory groups were formed to pilot the endeavor, one in a content area and one in a developmental area, corresponding with the NBPTS certification nomenclature. The first group was charged with developing standards for teachers of mathematics for children ranging from the early childhood through young adulthood developmental levels; the second was charged with developing standards for teachers of early adolescent children regardless of the specific content to be taught. Applications for advisory group members were then sought on a statewide basis. These groups were to develop the process for all remaining advisory groups. The use of pilots prior to full implementation of an action was to become a common board approach to developing components of the new preparation and licensing system.

One year after these initial steps were taken, the board approved a process for appointing the remaining 14 advisory groups, 3 to focus on standards for the remaining developmental levels and 11 to focus on standards for remaining content areas. A total of 575 responses were received from a statewide call for applications to fill 185 positions. Based on the work of the two pilot groups, an advisory group charge and an orientation were developed for the remaining groups. The standards development process approved by the board took 3 years to complete and included extensive dissemination of advisory group recommendations, followed by revisions based on feedback. As of June 1998, the board had adopted 17 sets of standards resulting from this process, which, in addition to the INTASC standards, would form the basis for the new preparation and licensing system. (An 18th set of standards is currently in draft form.) Although time consuming, the standards development process was to have important implications for the remaining work to be done on the new preparation and licensing system.

IMPLICATIONS OF THE BOARD'S STANDARDS DEVELOPMENT PROCESS

Advisory Group Charge and Composition

Whereas the current preparation and licensing system is highly segmented, and relationships between the various certificated areas have not been purposely drawn, the board sought to emphasize connections among the standards themselves and among the education professionals who were charged with developing and complying with the standards. In addition, whereas the current system, unlike systems for other professions, serves the purpose of credentialing rather than licensing (Pullin, 1998), the board sought to establish a true licensing system. In this system, licensure by the state would be differentiated from certification, which was to be bestowed by the profession through the NBPTS.

Thus, the groups were charged with defining the knowledge, dispositions, and performances that teachers need to practice responsibly when they enter teaching. All developmental and content standards were to be built on the INTASC foundation, linked to Indiana's prekindergarten through Grade 12 (P-12) standards, and consistent with the work of national learned societies and organizations. As a consequence of this charge, standards are highly interrelated as well as consistent with national professional standards and state standards for P-12 students.

The board also approved an advisory group composition that would encourage connections between teacher preparation curricula and classroom teaching. Each group had 10 members, one half of whom were P-12 school personnel. The remainder included higher education personnel, an IPSB board and staff member, and a consultant from the Indiana Department of Education.

Separating Developmental and Content Areas

Whereas the NBPTS framework focuses on content areas according to each developmental level, the board chose to separate the two by developing standards for content areas across developmental levels and standards for developmental levels across content areas. The intent was to portray how the same content area evolves as students move through the developmental areas as well as how students evolve as they move through developmental stages, once again emphasizing the connections that should be present in teacher preparation programs and in classroom practice. However, this separation of content and developmental levels has led to some confusion, since both educators and the public were accustomed to the traditional portrayal of grade-level-specific content. A board committee is currently developing a "comprehensive standards document," which hopefully will alleviate this confusion by displaying the connections among the standards for education professionals and with P-12 standards and national specialty group standards.

Using the National Board Framework Rather Than Existing Certification Areas for Developing the Standards

The original plan for developing the standards would have created standards advisory groups for every existing certification area. However, from the beginning, the board wished to reduce the number of areas to move to a true licensing system, that is, a system that would be enforceable through meaningful assessments, connected to the standards. In addition, the board wanted the new standards to reflect the continuum of professional development for education professionals as exemplified by the NCATE, INTASC, and NBPTS connections at the national level. Therefore, the board decided to begin its standards development work using the NBPTS certification framework as a guide. Although achieving the desired connections, the resulting standards implied that a number of traditional certification areas, such as gifted and talented education, journalism, business education, and others, would no longer be licensed. This situation has led the board to form another committee to determine which additional areas should be "licensed" and how standards for those areas will be recognized or developed.

Using External Standing Committees to Develop Administrator Standards

As noted earlier, the board's preparation and licensing authority encompasses teachers, administrators, and school services personnel. In Indiana, a unique arrangement has developed between the board and two education administrator organizations in the state that has enabled these organizations to take the lead in developing standards for the board's approval. In 1995, the Indiana Association of School Principals petitioned the board to form an external committee, to be operated and financed by that association, for the purpose of making recommendations to the board on matters concerning the preparation and licensure of building-level administrators. In response to this request, the board developed a process for external committee composition, appointment, and operations that complemented the board's advisory group process. The external committee approach has enabled the board to move more quickly on the development of standards for administrators and forged a strong productive relationship between the board and state-level administrator groups, which seemed unlikely during the board's early years of operation. Subsequently, an external committee was proposed by the Indiana Association of Public School Superintendents to develop standards for district-level administrators, which are currently in draft form and scheduled for board adoption in September 1999.

BUILDING THE "HOUSE"

By 1996, the standards development process was proceeding smoothly, and the board realized that it was time to move to the next steps in designing the new preparation and licensing system. Once again, in retreat format, the board deliberated with the help of its superintendent facilitator on the model that would guide the development of the system to institutionalize the new standards. To describe this model, we use the analogy of a house that has three floors and a roof. The first floor is the development of performance-based standards, the second floor is the design of assessments to determine if the standards are met, the third floor is the creation of a licensing configuration, and the roof is the enactment of statutes and rules necessary to implement the new system. Each floor has three rooms, representing the teacher development continuum of preparation, licensing, and continued professional growth through relicensing.

Implications of the House Model

In choosing this model, the board took a holistic approach to developing the new system, one that required careful attention to the order in which the "floors" would be built and ensuring that there were links between rooms and floors. Thus, although in previous times, specific credentialing areas were created first, followed by rules for preparation programs and selection of whichever tests might be available in the particular area, the new system would begin with standards, and competence in the standards would be assessed for licensing purposes. Only if standards and assessments based on the standards were developed would a license be granted in a specific teaching area. The house model also implies that a systemic approach was to be developed for preparation and licensure. Previously, various reform models addressed one or another component of the system, for example, 5-year preparation programs, or induction programs for beginning teachers, or new professional development strategies. In the board's model, all components would be addressed.

ACHIEVEMENTS TO DATE

Achieving Credibility/Serving as a Firewall

Over the past 7 years, the board has worked very hard to earn its reputation for fairness, thorough deliberation, and thoughtful decision making. Originally believed to be dominated by the teachers' associations, the board has earned the respect of all who work with it for its nonpartisan approach to getting the work done. In *What Matters Most: Teaching for America's Future*, the National Commission on Teaching & America's Future (NCTAF) (1996) suggests that autonomous professional standards boards can serve as a firewall between the political process and the standards-setting process. This has proven true in Indiana for the past 7 years in that no legislation has been passed that would negate the board's work thus far. However, in these times when the credibility of higher education, and of teacher education particularly, is in question, the ability of the standards board to "protect" all components of the profession is being severely challenged, as will be discussed below.

Bringing all Stakeholders to the Table on the Issue of Teacher Development

Until the board was established, there was little effort invested in coming to consensus on teacher knowledge and skills that should serve as the basis for preparation and licensure. Through its redesign of preparation and licensure, the board has involved hundreds of individuals representing all stakeholder groups in the education profession in the formulation of standards, assessments based on the standards, and a licensing framework that encompasses the standards and assessments. State-level associations, including the Indiana Association of Colleges for Teacher Education (IACTE), the Indiana Association of School Principals (IASP), the Indiana Association of Public School Superintendents (IAPSS), the Indiana State Teachers Association, and the Indiana Federation of Teachers, have been heavily involved in the board's work. The IACTE has worked cooperatively with the IPSB through several task forces and joint meetings. As mentioned earlier, both the IASP and the IAPSS have formed external subcommittees to work with the board on the redesigned system.

Realizing that preparation and licensing alone are insufficient to bring about the teacher development system desired by education professionals, the board submitted an application to the NCTAF to become a partner state. As one of 12 initial partner states, Indiana has formed an advisory council, encompassing more than 30 representatives from a broad variety of stakeholder groups, to address teacher development issues beyond teacher preparation and licensure.

System Redesign/Building the House

Due to the board's ability to focus solely on preparation and licensing issues, an incredible amount of work has been completed related to the board's new system. To return to the house analogy, work on the first floor, standards, is nearing completion. The board has yet to develop the process for reviewing, revising, and adding new sets of standards for licensure purposes.

With regard to the second floor, assessments, the board has been working since 1997, when it approved an assessment framework consisting of a staged licensure process to design and test specific assessment strategies for each licensure stage. The first stage in the licensure process requires teacher preparation institutions to develop standards-based curricula and assessments to ensure that teacher candidates have achieved an acceptable level of proficiency. Unit Assessment Systems, which document the curricula and candidate assessments to be used by teacher preparation programs, are to be submitted to the IPSB in 2002 for its approval by 2004. It is significant that the concept of the Unit Assessment System originated with a task force sponsored by the IACTE at the IPSB's request.

The original goal in moving to Unit Assessment Systems was to base state accreditation of teacher preparation programs and licensing decisions on reliable and credible assessment evidence showing that candidates recommended for initial licensure meet state standards. Candidate performance would be substituted for prescriptive course and credit hour requirements and the current norm-referenced paper-and-pencil tests used by the state for licensing purposes. According to Ingersoll and Scannell (1998), "In this manner, individual institutions would be able to interpret the IPSB standards in accord with their institutional missions and conceptual structure" (p. 7).

The board's original goal of eliminating the external paper-and-pencil tests once an assessment system had been approved has subsequently been determined to be premature given the as-yet-undeveloped nature of the Unit Assessment System. Given the political environment in the state (and nationally), board members were convinced that state legislators, who had imposed the testing requirements in the late 1980s, would not permit their elimination until credible and reliable evidence of candidates' performance had been submitted as a result of the new system. In addition, until institutional assessments can be implemented and candidate performance data are available, the tests can serve as one type of indicator of the quality of preparation programs and the institutions' assessment systems.

The IPSB's Teacher Education Committee has worked during the past 2 years to establish guidelines for institutions' assessment systems, a time line for the process, and criteria against which institutions would be evaluated. However, the specific review process, rubrics for scoring the systems, and benchmarks to provide guidance to institutions have yet to be developed. A major issue to be resolved by the board is how to ensure quality across the institutions while still enabling those institutions to develop assessment models that reflect their own missions and structures. It should be noted that although a course and credit hour structure never provided this kind of assurance, elimination of these requirements has prompted concerns about quality assurance among legislators and others. Another major issue for institutions, as a result of eliminating state-imposed course and credit hour requirements, will be developing the process for the transfer of students from one institution to another and from one program concentration to another. This will require that faculty within institutions understand how standards in the various licensing areas relate to each other and agree on and make public what students will know and be able to do as a result of teacher preparation program curricula.

The second stage in the licensure process involves the 2-year Beginning Teacher Induction Performance Assessment Program, patterned after a portfolio assessment developed by the INTASC and being implemented in Connecticut and now being piloted in Indiana, with a targeted startup date of 2001. The third stage in the new licensure process is relicensure on a 5- or 10-year basis, which can be accomplished by completing course work and/or professional growth experiences compatible with the teacher's Professional Growth Plan or by participating in the National Board Certification process. The 10-year license is achieved by earning National Board Certification or completing an advanced degree based on NBPTS and Indiana teacher standards. This stage is currently being piloted, with a projected startup date of 2002 for teachers needing to renew licenses in 2007. The Board's Licensure Framework, represented by the third floor of the house, was approved by the board in June 1999. To complete the house, rules will be developed and promulgated during 2000.

National Recognition

The board's careful process and involvement of all stakeholder groups has earned it national as well as state credibility. The NCTAF chose Indiana as one of its 13 partner states because of its work on teacher preparation and licensure. IPSB representatives have been asked to speak throughout the country by organizations and states wishing to emulate its new system design. In its 1998 publication, *Promising Practices*, the U.S. Department of Education featured Indiana's new performance-based system. The IPSB's Standards for Teachers of Middle Childhood are the only state standards cited within the standards portion of the draft *Program Standards for Elementary Teacher Preparation* (1998) developed by the NCATE's Elementary Program Standards Development Drafting Committee. Indiana is an acknowledged bellwether state in reforming teacher preparation and licensure.

PROBLEMS FACED

The board has enjoyed an extensive "honeymoon" period, 6 years of little interference from external groups, while working with education stakeholders to design the new system. It has become apparent during the past year that the honeymoon has ended as the board moves closer to system implementation. The enormity of the task ahead is daunting; however, the will of board members, several of whom have been involved since the board's inception, to move forward is equally impressive.

Getting to Scale

In his 1996 article, Richard Elmore discusses the difficult task of accomplishing systemwide educational reform. He states that "getting to scale with good education practice requires nothing less than deliberately creating and reproducing alternatives to the existing flawed institutional arrangements and incentive structures" (p. 25). The work of changing the institutional cultures of higher education, schools, and school districts is very difficult and requires stubborn persistence in the face of perceived stone walls and continuous movement forward over a long period of time. Unfortunately, persistence over time has not typically characterized educational reform in the United States, so we are fighting the odds.

Viewing Teaching as a Profession

As in other states, there are policy makers, members of the press, and members of the public who push for policies that suggest they do not believe that teaching is a complex activity, involving both knowledge of subject matter and knowledge of how to teach a particular subject and, the ability to put that knowledge into practice. Nor are they familiar with the growing knowledge base about teacher characteristics that lead to improved student learning. Finally, they reject any suggestion that members of the profession are the experts about who should teach and how they should be prepared.

Unfortunately, some members of the profession lend support to these doubts about the credibility of teachers and teacher educators by fighting for their own special interests rather than focusing on improving student learning and coalescing around policies that will lead to that end. The in-fighting among members of the profession in Indiana is expected to increase as the board implements its new system, which calls for significant changes in the traditional system, changes requiring real collaboration between higher education and P-12 educators and between teacher educators and liberal arts faculty and evidence that prospective teachers, beginning teachers, and practicing teachers are effective at improving student learning.

Resources—Time and Funding

Implementing the board's new system will require funding for teacher preparation programs, beginning teacher assessment and support, and continuing professional development. Thus far, this funding has been elusive. Although the Governor's Office has been very supportive of the work of the IPSB, and has promoted the IPSB's request for funds to implement the new standards and assessments, the legislature has not seen the merit of the new system and has not provided the necessary funding. This lack of support is in part the result of legislators' doubt that teacher preparation really makes a difference in student learning and in part the result of their doubt that the IPSB's new system will change that equation. We have a great deal to do to demonstrate that teacher preparation programs are necessary for producing effective teachers and can change to meet the needs of today's schools and students.

Events during the 1999 legislative session, originating with concerns that Indiana's teacher preparation institutions have not adequately prepared teachers to teach reading with a balanced set of methods (both phonics and whole language), have brought these problems to the forefront and challenge all members of the teaching profession, representing teacher preparation and P-12 systems, to demonstrate their relevance to student learning and willingness to be held accountable for their practice.

Related Teacher Development Issues and Lack of Empirical Evidence

Typically, when explaining the board's new system to a group of educators, questions abound with regard to low teacher pay, lack of time and funding, and existing and anticipated teacher shortages. These are also issues of concern to the board but not within the board's power to solve. Only through a coalition of stakeholder groups, such as the Indiana Advisory Council for the NCTAF partnership, can the broader issues beyond teacher preparation and licensure be addressed.

It is easier to find the reasons why the new system will not work than to undertake the changes the board's new system will require. In addition to the difficulty of undertaking change, there is as yet little empirical evidence that a standards-based teacher preparation and licensing system will make a difference. Thus, we are asking education stakeholder groups to take a leap of faith based primarily on the rationality of connecting teacher standards to student standards and holding all participants accountable for meeting those standards. We are beginning to see some evidence supporting the importance of teacher characteristics to student learning (NCTAF, 1997) and the impact of standards-based teaching (Connecticut State Department of Education, 1998); however, the evidence has not yet convinced a sufficient number of policy makers, teacher educators, and teachers in Indiana that moving to a standards-based system is worth the investment of the substantial time and funds it requires.

Being on the Cutting Edge

In Indiana, we are developing systems, particularly for teacher preparation program and relicensure assessments, that are on the cutting edge. As a result, all of the answers are not evident, there must be trial and error, and transitions are difficult. In a culture where risk taking is not rewarded, change is frightening, and unknowns are not acceptable, it is easier to return to the old, known ideas than to develop solutions to the unknowns.

Being a Change Agent and a State Agency May Well Be an Oxymoron

Although state governmental processes in Indiana are beginning to change, their design often serves to prevent rather than facilitate change. The paperwork required and the number of agencies involved in each transaction consumes both time and staff resources that could otherwise be devoted to developing new, more efficient and responsive systems. Personnel salary structures and reward systems discourage the best and brightest from applying for positions and from staying very long if they do work for the state. Limits on numbers of employees an agency may employ and a cumbersome process for contracting with consultants make it difficult to assume the role of change agent while continuing to meet ongoing customer needs. In spite of the support of the Governor's Office and some of the state agencies, the IPSB staff continues to struggle with these constraints.

CONCLUSION

These are daunting challenges; however, we believe they can be met. The history of the IPSB demonstrates board members' willingness to pursue best practice in spite of the odds. The support of most teacher preparation institutions; teachers', principals', and superintendents' associations; and the Governor's Office also gives reason to anticipate that Indiana can maintain its steady progress toward the reform of teacher preparation and licensure. What is needed now is for these groups to come together to convince legislators, business representatives, and the public that their support for the board's redesigned system, not simplistic approaches such as requiring more courses or alternative licensing systems, will make a difference in student learning.

REFERENCES

Connecticut State Department of Education. (1998). *Impact: Summary of findings of impact of BEST Program on Student Achievement.* Unpublished manuscript.

Elmore, R. (1996). Getting to scale with good educational practice. *Harvard Educational Review, 66*(1), 1-26.

Indiana Code, Title 20, Education, Article 1, Chapter 1.4, Section 2, Professional Standards Board (1998).

Ingersoll, G., & Scannell, D. (1998). Performance-based teacher preparation and licensure. *Quality Teaching, 7*(2), 6-8.

Interstate New Teacher Assessment and Support Consortium. (1992, September). *Model standards for beginning teacher licensing and development: A resource for state dialogue.* Washington, DC: Author.

National Commission on Teaching & America's Future. (1996, September). *What matters most: Teaching for America's future.* New York: Author.

National Commission on Teaching & America's Future. (1997, November). *Doing what matters most: Investing in quality teaching.* New York: Author.

National Council for Accreditation of Teacher Education. (1998, September). *Program standards for elementary teacher preparation. Review and comment edition.* Washington, DC: Author.

Pullin, D. C. (1998). *Reforms in standards-based teacher education, certification, and licensure: Legal issues in implementation* (Report prepared for the Interstate New Teacher Assessment and Support Consortium). Washington, DC: Council of Chief State School Officers.

U.S. Department of Education. (1998). *Promising practices: New ways to improve teacher quality.* Washington, DC: Author.

The Georgia Story of
P-16 Partnerships

JAN S. KETTLEWELL, JANINE A. KASTE,
and SHEILA A. JONES

This article recounts accomplishments of state and local P-16 partnerships toward improving teacher quality, raising educational aspirations, and improving student achievement. Work on teacher quality is emphasized, and a plan is in place for having a qualified teacher in every public school classroom by 2006. Although primary, work on teacher quality is insufficient. It must be coupled with efforts to raise and align academic standards for students, preschool through postsecondary education.

THE GEORGIA Pre-School–Post-Secondary Education (P-16) Initiative began in 1995. It was a time ripe for change with the commitment of top leadership and with widespread agreement in the state as to the need to increase student achievement to desired levels. Educational aspirations in Georgia

AUTHORS' NOTE: The authors acknowledge that the work described here represents the contributions of many groups and individuals. In particular, the authors wish to acknowledge the work of the following: The Georgia P-16 Council; the Executive Committee of the Teachers and Teacher Education P-16 Subcommittee; the 15 local P-16 councils; Jacqueline Michael, director of Pre-College Programs for the University System and the coordinators at each of the 25 colleges and universities participating in the Post-Secondary Readiness Enrichment Program; Peyton Williams, deputy state school superintendent and cofacilitator of the Georgia P-16 Initiative for the Department of Education; Judy Monsaas, faculty associate from North Georgia College and State University and coordinator of evaluation for the Georgia P-16 Initiative; Dorothy Zinsmeister, senior associate in academic affairs; and Lana Blackwell, administrative associate for the Georgia P-16 Initiative.

EDUCATIONAL POLICY, Vol. 14 No. 1, January and March 2000 77-92
© 2000 Corwin Press, Inc.

were not sufficiently high. At all levels of public education, preschool through postsecondary, problems of underachievement persisted.

Within the K-12 sector, Georgia scores were (and remain) lower on the National Assessment on Educational Progress (NAEP) than the national averages and the states in the Southeast that have been making the most significant improvements. From 1990 to 1997, enrollment growth in Georgia's public schools has been increasing at a faster rate (17%) than average increases in the Unites States (12%) and Southern Regional Education Board (SREB) states (12%). In 1995, according to SREB (1998) data, Georgia also had a higher percentage of students from minority groups (42%) than either the United States as a whole (35%) or SREB states (35%). Population increases (projected to continue) were and are likely to exacerbate the challenges Georgia's public schools face to increase student achievement to desired levels.

Within the postsecondary sector, about 40% of first-time freshmen in the University System (all public 2-year colleges and universities in Georgia) required learning support (remedial education), and close to 30% of these students had completed the college preparatory curriculum in high school (Hudson, Whitman, & Marshall, 1997). About 20% of high school graduates entering postsecondary technical institutes scored below "program ready" on one or more of the tests required for admission (writing, reading, and numerical skills). Likewise, employers who hire high school graduates reported that high school graduates were unprepared for work (Georgia P-16 Council, 1997).

Clearly, a comprehensive strategy was needed to address these problems throughout all levels of public education in Georgia. The challenge was to select those levers that held the greatest promise for raising student aspirations and increasing the level of student achievement, preschool through postsecondary education. Drawing on the work of the Education Trust (a nonprofit organization created to promote high academic achievement for all students at all levels), the Georgia P-16 Initiative was initiated as a primary comprehensive strategy to raise student aspirations and the levels of educational achievement from preschool (P) through postsecondary education (16).

THE GEORGIA P-16 INITIATIVE

The Georgia P-16 Initiative was initiated by the Board of Regents of the University System of Georgia at a time when the board was raising admission requirements in all public colleges and universities in the state. In July 1995, Governor Zell Miller created the Georgia P-16 Council and charged the members with improving the academic achievement of students at all levels.

During the first meeting of the council, Governor Miller emphasized that "the only way that this can happen is if our schools, colleges and technical institutes work together." He charged the council with serving as an advocate for P-16 reform by recommending local and state educational policy aimed at strengthening the relationships between the educational systems, the business community, and other youth advocate organizations.

During the first implementation phase of P-16, the governor appointed an executive committee to map out the council's initial focus and structure. The executive committee swiftly completed its work and disbanded. Based on the recommendations of the executive committee, a senior advocacy group was charged with creating the initial P-16 agenda. The Georgia P-16 Council approved the following agenda in 1996:

1. Development of standards of what students should know and be able to do beginning in preschool and continuing through postsecondary levels;
2. Creation of a P-16 multiagency-linked student database to monitor student progress through all levels of education;
3. Alignment of curricula from preschool through postsecondary education;
4. Strengthening teacher quality through the co-reform of schools and preparation programs for teachers, school leaders, and educational support personnel.

Currently, the Georgia P-16 Council is cochaired through a rotation system of the four heads of the Office of School Readiness (Georgia's voluntary preschool program), the State Department of Education, the Department of Technical and Adult Education, and the University System. The council includes individuals from postsecondary education, P-12 education, the legislature, youth advocate groups, the corporate sector, and the community. The council meets four times per year and has 49 members, with the governor serving as honorary chair. Georgia's P-16 Council provides overall coordination and leadership for the P-16 Initiative at state and local levels. Subcommittees are appointed to carry out the work of the council. Subcommittee recommendations are then forwarded to the council for action. Because the council is not a governance structure with any authority in policy or law, recommendations approved are forwarded to the proper authorities and governing boards.

The mission of the Georgia P-16 Initiative is to improve student success (Georgia P-16 Council, 1996). There are three strands of work:

1. Alignment of expectations (standards), curricula, and assessment for students, preschool through postsecondary education;

2. Alignment of school reform and teacher preparation reform toward practices that improve student learning in P-12 schools (co-reform);
3. Supplemental programs for 7th- through 12th-grade students in at-risk situations who would benefit from extra support to be prepared for postsecondary education.

Early on, it was recognized that work at the state level, although necessary, was insufficient. Local partnerships were needed to provide the infrastructure necessary to build grassroots support and pilot new directions. In 1997, using University System funds as seed money, 15 local/regional P-16 councils were formed in Georgia. Each council received $10,000 and was charged with development of unique plans to achieve the P-16 mission through focusing on one or more of the three strands of work. The membership within the 15 local P-16 councils soon included the following participants: 29 University System colleges and universities (out of 34), 147 school districts (out of 180), 23 technical institutes (out of 34), 23 private schools, 80 businesses, 41 public agencies, and representatives from communities.

The 15 local P-16 councils now constitute the Georgia P-16 network and meet regularly to focus on local, regional, or statewide needs. The network serves as a vehicle for maintaining close communication and building cross-regional relationships between participants. Using funds from the University System, the state of Georgia, and the private sector, local councils have had opportunities to compete for challenge grants to implement their plans in either or both of the first two strands of work listed above. Eighteen multiyear challenge grants have been awarded to local councils to date.

In 2001, the University System's new admission requirements will go into effect. The third strand of work within the P-16 initiative is intended to help students in the pipeline who may not be prepared to meet the higher requirements. The Post-Secondary Readiness Enrichment Program (PREP) was thus implemented in 1996 as a supplemental academic program offered to 7th- through 12th-grade students in at-risk situations to facilitate their access to postsecondary education. Using matching state and private funding, school-postsecondary partnerships had an opportunity to implement PREP. Twenty colleges and universities within the University System, 20 technical institutes, and 178 schools organized into nine collaborative sites to offer PREP services. PREP services include special advising to get students into more rigorous courses, homework assistance, tutoring, mentoring, career exploration, leadership development, cultural enrichment, community service, and parental involvement.

PREP began offering services to seventh graders during the 1996-1997 school year. Each year, a class is retained and the new seventh graders are added. This program is helping close the gap for students in at-risk situations and is scheduled to end in its present form in 2001 when the new admission requirements go into effect.

WORK AT THE STATE LEVEL ON
TEACHER PREPARATION

In 1996, the Georgia P-16 Council targeted teacher quality as a priority. A Teachers and Teacher Education P-16 Subcommittee was appointed to (a) assess what needed to change in Georgia to improve teacher quality and (b) develop recommendations for change. During the early work of this subcommittee, Georgia became a partner state with the National Commission on Teaching & America's Future (NCTAF) (1996). The Teachers and Teacher Education Subcommittee became the council's action arm for carrying out Georgia's participation as a partner state with the NCTAF.

Early work of the Teachers and Teacher Education P-16 Subcommittee resulted in

- an overall framework for change
- recommendations to increase the availability of alternative teacher preparation programs and strengthen traditional programs
- completion of *The Status of Teaching in Georgia* (Teachers and Teacher Education P-16 Subcommittee, 1998), a state report on the status of each of the recommendations of the NCTAF.

The Professional Standards Commission (Georgia's Teacher Certification Agency) and Board of Regents (governing board for all public colleges and universities in Georgia) took immediate action on these recommendations. In 1997, the Professional Standards Commission put in place the Innovative Program Rule to expand alternative teacher preparation programs, and in 1998, the commission approved the first alternative teacher preparation program. Following a full year of study, the Board of Regents adopted a 1998 Policy on Teacher Preparation for all public universities that prepare teachers, and for FY 2000, the Georgia General Assembly appropriated $3 million to assist with implementation. The regents' 1998 policy culminates in a "guarantee" for the quality of new teachers, effective 2004. The guarantee is summarized as follows:

1. Subject matter knowledge of sufficient depth to enable teachers to help P-12 students from diverse groups to reach high academic standards and to learn for understanding.

2. Demonstrated effective use of information and telecommunication technologies as tools for learning during the internship.
3. Demonstrated success during the internship in bringing students from diverse cultural, ethnic, international, and socioeconomic groups to high levels of learning.
4. Managed a classroom effectively during the internship.
5. Demonstrated success during the internship in early childhood programs in diagnosing difficulties in reading and mathematics and helping students show improvement.
6. Following graduation, the teacher preparing institution will provide additional training for the teacher, at no cost to the school or the teacher, if the teacher does not meet the school's expectations. If needed, the additional training will be individualized and desired learning outcomes specified.

Building on these accomplishments of the Professional Standards Commission and the Board of Regents, the Georgia P-16 Council charged the Teachers and Teacher Education P-16 Subcommittee with the development of a comprehensive plan of steps necessary to have a qualified teacher in every public school classroom by 2006. The Georgia P-16 Council approved this plan in June 1999.

WORK AT THE LOCAL LEVEL ON TEACHER QUALITY

Many dimensions of work on teacher quality at the state level within the Board of Regents and the Georgia P-16 Council originated within the 15 local P-16 councils that have been working on two of the three strands of P-16 work:

- Alignment of expectations (standards), curriculum, and assessment for students, preschool through postsecondary education
- Alignment of school reform and teacher preparation reform toward practices that improve student learning in P-12 schools (co-reform).

Since 1997, an annual request for proposals has been distributed to local P-16 councils, asking for implementation plans and documented results in these two strands of work. Those councils awarded challenge grants evidenced in their proposals systemic actions and measurable outcomes that focused on improving student success. Currently, six councils hold dual grants of $200,000 or $150,000 each, and another six councils hold one grant of $200,000 or $150,000 over 3 years, to work on alignment and/or co-reform. Three of the councils are still refining implementation plans.

Initiatives within local P-16 councils that focus on teacher quality include creating "functional units" of faculty from the arts and sciences, education, and partner schools to be responsible for teacher preparation; establishing teacher preparation standards; redesigning courses that prepare new teachers with adequate subject matter knowledge to teach diverse learners; and developing partner schools.

Functional Units

Through the work of local P-16 councils, university faculty from the arts and sciences and education and school faculty from partner schools have increased collaboration and are developing shared responsibility for teacher preparation. This work within local P-16 councils informed the development of state policy within the University System of Georgia. The Board of Regents' 1998 Policy on the Preparation of Educators for the Schools requires each public university that prepares teachers to identify the group of faculty to be responsible for the quality of teacher preparation from among the arts and sciences, education, and the schools and organize these faculty members into a functional unit (Georgia Board of Regents, 1998). These functional units are analogous to Centers of Pedagogy promoted by John Goodlad (1990) through the National Network for Educational Renewal. Patterson, Michelli, and Pacheco (1999) describe Georgia as the only state with established policy that formalizes the tripartite partnership (arts and sciences, education, and school faculty) responsible for the preparation of teachers.

Teacher Education Standards

Three local P-16 councils are participating in the Standards-Based Teacher Education Project (STEP), a project funded by the Council for Basic Education and the American Association of Colleges for Teacher Education. The project aims to bridge the gap between course content in teacher preparation programs and what new teachers are expected to teach students in the classroom (i.e., P-12 academic standards). It also aims to bridge what is covered in college courses on content and pedagogy instruction and the teaching strategies that new teachers are expected to use in the classroom. This program includes the education, arts and sciences, and school faculty who are responsible for the preparation of teachers.

Henry and Kettlewell (in press) describe how STEP has developed within the Metropolitan Atlanta P-16 Council:

A subcommittee of faculty members from various departments was established to analyze the alignment of content courses and program requirements in the mathematics teacher preparation programs with the Metropolitan Atlanta P-16 draft Voluntary Academic Standards in mathematics. Analyses of mathematics content were to cover programs at all levels: early childhood education (P-5), middle school education (4-8), and secondary education (8-12). Thus the subcommittee examined benchmark standards at levels 5, 8, and 12, and developed a draft of analyses of the sufficiency or insufficiency of the coverage of academic content for the early childhood, middle school, and secondary level programs. After discussion and refinement by the STEP Task Force, the subcommittee findings and recommendations were sent to all the relevant departments for comment. The next step in the current process is to determine what, if any, modifications in courses or programs are necessary in order to ensure that student teachers will be proficient in the subjects they will be expected to teach. In addition to mathematics, subcommittees have been set up in the sciences, English/language arts, and social studies. As work progresses, it is the intent to begin to incorporate art, music, foreign language, school counseling, and special education into the STEP activities. In addition to much stronger content preparation programs for new educators, the approach in the Standards-based Teacher Education Project can be used to provide more relevant and focused professional development for in-service educators.

Redesigning Courses

Through collaboration, university and P-12 faculty have redesigned teacher preparation course work to meet more effectively the needs of the diverse learners new teachers will encounter in the classroom. One such opportunity between a university and one of its partner middle schools resulted in a new field-based reading methods block of courses for prospective teachers (Many & Elliot, in press). Reading/language arts faculty from both the middle school and the university came together to discuss how to prepare middle grades prospective teachers to meet the needs of the struggling readers in the middle school. This dialogue informed the design of a course, taught at the middle school, that included a field-based opportunity for prospective teachers to tutor struggling middle school students. Thus, prospective teachers implemented and reflected on the effectiveness of instructional strategies and assessment tools that traditionally were taught at the university without the opportunity for direct practice.

Partner Schools

Within many of the local P-16 councils, universities that prepare teachers and area schools are joining together to develop partner schools. These partner schools focus concurrently on improving student learning in the school, providing more meaningful and authentic field experiences for prospective teachers, cooperating in professional development of school and university faculty, and collaborating in research aimed at strengthening both the school and teacher preparation. Through partner schools, former program assignments are replaced with ones that meet more effectively what actually occurs in the classroom (Thornton, Eisenman, & Gendernalik-Cooper, in press), and classroom teachers bring classroom practice to the university, as adjunct faculty in undergraduate programs (Jamerson, in press). University faculty also benefit from day-to-day participation in the schools. The children benefit from the whole school emphasis on strengthening student learning.

Moving Toward Accountability

The Regents' 1998 Policy for the Preparation of Educators for the Schools requires public universities that prepare teachers to move to new levels of accountability. Beginning in 2004 as a precondition to graduation and recommendation for certification, teacher candidates must be able to demonstrate accomplishment in bringing students from diverse groups to high levels of learning. The overall direction of this policy is to shift from a primary focus on "inputs" (courses, credit hours, number of clock hours of student internships in schools) to "results" (teacher, counselor, and administrator candidates able to show accomplishment in bringing about increased learning of children in the schools). Although it is recognized that inputs and teacher or administrator performance remain important enablers of effectiveness, the primary emphasis is the following: All those recommended for teacher certification must be able to demonstrate success in bringing students from diverse groups to high levels of learning (Georgia Board of Regents, 1998).

SUPPORTING RESEARCH

When one considers the numerous examples of educational reform initiatives that have been attempted but produced little results, it is clear that neither top-down nor bottom-up strategies are sufficient. Both are needed. Large-scale systemic change involves collaboration and networking between all participants and the alteration of current systemic conditions that define learning and teaching (Fullan, 1993, 1994). As Fullan (1996) eloquently states,

Systems have a better track record of maintaining the status quo than they have of changing themselves. This is why attempting to change the system directly, through regulation and structural reform, does not work. It is people who change systems, through the development of new critical masses. Once a critical mass becomes a majority, we begin to see the system change. The lesson of systemic reform is to look for those strategies that are most likely to mobilize large numbers of people in new directions. Evaluation should focus on this development, not because it will always result in clear measures, but because such a focus will propel the very changes essential for systemic breakthroughs. (p. 423)

Thus, successful reform requires both the effort and commitment of state and local participants and the involvement of all stakeholders who contribute to the preparation of new teachers—education faculty, P-12 faculty, and arts and sciences faculty. It is these people who can best plan and implement courses of action and assess progress. It is why Georgia's P-16 Initiative recognizes the importance of allocating resources that support both broad and local efforts to meet desired goals.

Use of a comprehensive P-16 strategy to improve student learning is well documented (Education Trust, 1996, 1997; State Higher Education Executive Offices, 1998). The 1994 report of the American Federation of Teachers summed it up the following way:

Colleges and universities train our public school teachers and conduct the nation's research on teaching and learning. Through their admissions policies, colleges and universities exert a powerful influence on the content of the public school curriculum and on the courses taken by students who aspire to a college education. For school reform to work, higher education must become a full partner. For higher education to advance, the schools must become stronger. (p. 3)

Beyond support in the literature for P-16's infrastructure, there is a growing body of research that documents teacher quality as the most important factor in student achievement (Ferguson, 1991; Thomas-Armour, Clay, Domanico, Bruno, & Allen, 1989). Research also supports the idea that to effect positive student achievement, teachers must possess both strong content knowledge and pedagogy (Darling-Hammond, 1996; Ferguson, 1991; Goodlad, 1990; NCTAF, 1997; Sikula, Buttery, & Guyton, 1996; Thomas-Armour et al., 1989). In particular, they must be aware of the diverse abilities, prior knowledge, and experiences of their learners to foster optimal learning (Resnick, 1987). The students of those teachers who hold higher teacher qualifications and are teaching within their field of certification rank higher on NAEP reading and math assessments (NCTAF, 1997). Use of partner schools, also featured in Georgia's P-16 Initiative, is based on the research of Goodlad (1990, 1994) and his colleagues at the Center for Educational Renewal.

A key emphasis in Georgia's P-16 strategy requires all teachers recommended for certification (new and continuing) to show accomplishment in bringing students from diverse groups to high levels of learning. Schalock (1996) has completed most of the research documenting the success of this strategy in initial teacher preparation. Using a technique called the "work sample methodology," Schalock's research supports the idea that new teachers can be held to high standards in "What they know and are able to do" + "What they can accomplish in promoting student learning."

LESSONS LEARNED

An Early Lesson Learned in Georgia

P-16 partnerships help school and university faculty imagine greater possibilities and more out-of-the-box thinking than either imagines alone. By bringing P-16 groups together from various regions of the state and sharing the work of Goodlad, Darling-Hammond, and others, teams recognize the need for building local structures to achieve the P-16 mission. At the state level, P-16 partnerships create the infrastructure necessary to build an integrated policy framework for improving teacher quality and for monitoring student learning across the various educational sectors. The P-16 initiative increases the probability that all key stakeholders are pulling in the same direction.

A Second Lesson Learned in Georgia

Work on improving teacher quality will fall short of desired expectations unless it is coupled with systematic efforts to align academic standards for students, preschool through college. In most states, there are gaps between what students know and are able to do when they graduate from high school and what they need to know and be able to do to succeed in college. There are also gaps between the academic standards demanded in schools for P-12 students and the content knowledge teachers bring to the task.

Much work is under way in teacher preparation nationwide to align the content knowledge of prospective teachers with P-12 academic standards for students. Less is being done to ensure high school graduates will be ready to succeed in college if they meet the level 12 standards. It has been our experience that academic and performance standards for P-12 students will be set and assessed at higher levels when they are developed within a P-16 context. If these higher standards are then used to set content knowledge standards for teachers, chances are greater that both gaps identified in the preceding paragraph can be closed.

A Third Lesson Learned in Georgia

Resources do make a difference. Through various grant opportunities and local, state, and national meeting opportunities, local councils have found ways to make a difference in all strands of P-16 work. In teacher quality, councils throughout the state have expanded partnerships among colleges of arts and sciences, education, and P-12 schools. Functional units (identified groups of faculty from the arts and sciences, education, and partner schools with responsibility for teacher preparation) are in place or under development. P-12 teachers are emerging as collaborative partners in all types of field experiences for preservice teachers and in providing instruction at the college level. There is evidence that with increased frequency, school and university faculties are engaging in cooperative professional development and research.

A Fourth Lesson Learned in Georgia

The belief that all children can learn at high levels has widened. The next challenge is to implement comprehensive strategies for realizing this belief. The highest priority is to place a qualified teacher in every public school classroom in Georgia and raise the bar on what is meant by a qualified teacher.

CHALLENGES AND NEXT STEPS

Consistent with the recommendations of the NCTAF (1996), Georgia envisions having a qualified teacher in every public school classroom by 2006. The Georgia P-16 Council has defined a qualified teacher as one who knows all of the subjects he or she teaches and is successful in helping students from diverse groups achieve at high levels. Georgia's plan for achieving this vision includes two goals and eight objectives (Georgia P-16 Council, 1999). The goals are the following:

1. To improve the quality of teaching in Georgia through comprehensive and integrative changes in teacher recruitment, teacher preparation, teacher standards (initial certification and renewal every 5 years), teacher professional development, and teacher retention.
2. To improve student achievement in Georgia's schools through improving the quality of teaching.

The objectives are the following:

1. Balance teacher supply and demand in all subject fields, grade levels, and geographic regions of the state.
2. Decrease teacher attrition during first 3 years of teaching.
3. End out-of-field teaching in all subject fields and grade levels.

4. Change certification standards to require new teachers and current teachers to demonstrate success in bringing students from diverse groups to high levels of learning.
5. Raise admission requirements into teacher preparation programs.
6. Strengthen the content knowledge requirements for new teachers of all subject fields and grade levels.
7. Focus teacher professional development and graduate degrees for teachers more directly on content knowledge and practices that improve student learning in schools.
8. Increase accountability for the quality of teaching and for improved student achievement in Georgia's schools.

When all eight objectives are achieved, Georgia will have reached the first goal. The second goal is predicated on the first goal. Student achievement must drive all actions to improve teacher quality. Student achievement in Georgia will increase proportionately with our success in improving teacher quality. This premise is consistent with the research of the NCTAF (1997) and Darling-Hammond (1996).

Georgia's plan describes identified needs and intended actions to achieve each objective. Stakeholders responsible for making each change have been identified. Time lines and points of accountability have been set. The evidence that will be accepted to indicate satisfactory progress at each milepost in our journey has been identified. A management team has been assembled to oversee implementation of Georgia's plan. The Teachers and Teacher Education P-16 Subcommittee has agreed to serve as the advisory council to the management team throughout implementation of the plan. The management team will present periodic progress reports to the heads of the public education agencies in meetings of the Georgia P-16 Council. The expectation is that progress reports will focus on outcomes rather than plans (Georgia P-16 Council, 1999).

Georgia's plan for having a qualified teacher in every public school classroom requires tightening the connections between current policies and ensuring they are pulling in the same direction. Georgia's plan also requires additional policy to be developed in the following areas:

- to balance teacher supply and demand;
- to end out-of-field teaching;
- to tie teacher certification to teacher success in bringing students from diverse groups to high levels of learning and to require induction programs for all new teachers;

- to focus teacher professional development directly on improving student achievement;
- to put conditions in place in schools that support teacher success in improving student learning, including reduced class size; and
- to strengthen accountability for the quality of teaching and for student learning in Georgia's public schools (Georgia P-16 Council, 1999).

Georgia's plan includes an integrated phase-in of all elements of a policy framework to ensure that local schools, colleges, and universities have the resources, support, and assistance to implement current and proposed policies. The plan provides for the P-16 partners at the state level to work collaboratively in offering incentives and targeted assistance to help public schools (particularly schools that have been designated as consistently low performing) and universities develop the capacity to reach the eight objectives. Following adoption of a new policy on accountability, the P-16 partners will put in place the necessary measures to ensure compliance. State report cards on teacher preparation and on Georgia's teaching force will be used to show progress toward our first goal of improving teacher quality. Progress toward our second goal will be monitored in tandem with the first (Georgia P-16 Council, 1999).

The Georgia P-16 Initiative is a comprehensive, long-term strategy. Components of the initiative that emphasize teacher preparation and teacher quality have been emphasized here. Work on the alignment of expectations for students, curriculum, and assessment; preschool-postsecondary education; and PREP represent equally powerful and necessary levers for raising educational aspirations and reducing underachievement of Georgia's students. All three strands of work are necessary to achieve the P-16 mission: "Students meet high standards and demonstrate achievement at each level, and are ready for the next level, whether that next level is work, technical training, or education, resulting in productive employment and responsible citizenship" (Georgia P-16 Council, 1996).

REFERENCES

American Federation of Teachers College-School Task Force on Student Achievement. (1994). *Closing the circle: Making higher education a full partner in systemic reform* [Online]. Washington, DC: American Federation of Teachers.

Darling-Hammond, L. (1996). What matters most: A competent teacher for every child. *Phi Delta Kappan, 78,* 193-200.

Education Trust. (1996). *Education watch: The 1996 Education Trust state and national book.* Washington, DC: Author.

Education Trust. (1997). *Education watch: The 1997 Education Trust state and national book.* Washington, DC: Author.

Ferguson, R. (1991). Paying for public education: New evidence on how and why money matters. *Harvard Journal on Legislation, 28,* 465-498.

Fullan, M. (1993). *Change forces: Probing the depths of educational reform.* Bristol, PA: Falmer.

Fullan, M. (1994). Coordinating top-down and bottom-up strategies for educational reform. In S. Fuhrman & R. Elmore (Eds.), *The governance of curriculum* (pp. 186-202). Alexandria, VA: Association for Supervision and Curriculum Development.

Fullan, M. (1996). Turning systemic thinking on its head. *Phi Delta Kappan, 77,* 420-423.

Georgia Board of Regents, University System of Georgia. (1998). *The Board of Regents' 1998 policy on the preparation of educators for the schools* [Online]. Available: www.usg.edu/p16/teachprep

Georgia P-16 Council. (1996, January). *State P-16 council meeting minutes.* Atlanta: Board of Regents of the University System of Georgia, Academic Affairs.

Georgia P-16 Council. (1997, December). *State P-16 council meeting minutes.* Atlanta: Board of Regents of the University System of Georgia, Academic Affairs.

Georgia P-16 Council (1999, June). *Georgia's plan for having a qualified teacher in every public classroom by 2006* [Online]. Available: www.sug.edu/p16/teachprep

Goodlad, J. I. (1990). *Teachers for our nation's schools.* San Francisco: Jossey-Bass.

Goodlad, J. I. (1994). *Educational renewal.* San Francisco: Jossey-Bass.

Henry, R., & Kettlewell, J. (in press). Georgia P-16 Initiative: Local partnerships within states. *Metropolitan Universities.*

Hudson, C., Whitman, S., & Marshall, A. (Eds.). (1997). *University System of Georgia enrollment reports* (1997 University System of Georgia Information Digest). Atlanta, GA: Board of Regents.

Jamerson, J. (in press). Georgia Southern University's demonstration teacher program: Insights from one demonstration teacher. *Georgia P-16 in Action, 1*(1).

Many, J., & Elliott, L. (in press). Listening to the voices of co-reform: A partnership develops a field-based reading methods course. *Georgia P-16 in Action.*

National Commission on Teaching & America's Future. (1996). *What matters most: Teaching for America's future.* New York: Author.

National Commission on Teaching & America's Future. (1997). *Doing what matters most: Investing in quality teaching.* New York: Author.

Patterson, R., Michelli, N., & Pacheco, A. (1999). *Centers of pedagogy.* San Francisco: Jossey-Bass.

Resnick, L. B. (1987). *Education and learning to think.* Washington, DC: National Academy Press.

Schalock, D. (1996). *Teacher effectiveness project.* Oregon: Western Oregon University, Teaching Research Division of the School of Education.

Sikula, J., Buttery, T., & Guyton, E. (Eds.). (1996). *Handbook of research on teacher education* (2nd ed.). New York: Association of Teacher Educators.

Southern Region Education Board. (1998). *Educational benchmarks 1998: Individual state data report.* Atlanta, GA: Author.

State Higher Education Executive Offices. (1998). *State strategies that support successful student transitions from secondary to post-secondary education.* Denver, CO: State Higher Education Executive Office.

Teachers and Teacher Education P-16 Subcommittee. (1998, March). *The status of teaching in Georgia.* Atlanta: Board of Regents, University System of Georgia.

Thomas-Armour, E., Clay, C., Domanico, R., Bruno, K., & Allen, B. (1989). *An outlier study of elementary and middle schools in New York City: Final report.* New York: New York City Board of Education.

Thornton, H., Eisenman, G., & Gendernalik-Cooper. (in press). Building a lasting collaborative: The professional development school initiative of the Central Savannah River Area P-16 Council. *Georgia P-16 in Action, 1*(1), 10-12.

Part 3

A Story From the Urban Arena

The Language of Standards and Teacher Education Reform

ROBERT J. YINGER
and MARTHA S. HENDRICKS-LEE

The key to successful professionalization of any practice is to convince clients and the public that a professional, as a result of education and practical experience, possesses unique knowledge and skills that can be employed to solve the particular problems of practice and thus serve client needs. Research and knowledge-based standards can convey the professional qualifications of teachers by creating a shared and public language of practice that not only describes how knowledge is used in practice but also becomes a vehicle for testing and elaborating the components of professional activity. Standards, when used in this manner by a developing profession, thus become a means to development and empowerment, not merely a means of external control.

STANDARDS HAVE BECOME a regular feature of the political landscape in education. Many state legislatures see standards as the means for improving all components of the educational system, from standards for student achievement, standards for teacher preparation programs, and standards for teacher induction through standards for advanced professional certification. At the same time, educators view standards primarily as a threat, as external controls aimed at dictating or controlling practice. Our purpose in this article is to move beyond the political tug-of-war that standards are perceived to create and to argue for standards as a powerful tool in the development of teaching as a profession.

Here is our argument in a nutshell. The key to successful professionalization of any practice is to convince clients and the public that a professional, as a result of education and practical experience, possesses unique knowledge

EDUCATIONAL POLICY, Vol. 14 No. 1, January and March 2000 94-106

and skills that can be employed to solve the particular problems of practice and thus serve client needs. This "legitimization" process depends greatly on a profession's ability to create a body of useful abstract knowledge that can be effectively converted to particular solutions in particular contexts. For this knowledge base to be created, a discourse language must be created that connects abstract knowledge and theory to the demands and realities of practice. Research and knowledge-based standards can serve in this manner by creating a shared and public "language of practice" (Yinger, 1987) that not only describes how knowledge is used in practice but also becomes a vehicle for testing and elaborating the components of professional activity. Standards, when used in this manner by a developing profession, thus become a means to development and empowerment, not merely a means of external control.

THE THREAT OF STANDARDS

At one level, the threat of standards is very real. States such as Texas and Ohio plan to or have already implemented high-stakes accountability for student performance, school performance, teacher performance, and performance of teacher education programs. Potential sanctions for not meeting standards include students not graduating or not being promoted, schools being reconstituted, districts being taken over by the state, teachers being denied licensure, and the closing of teacher preparation programs.

From the public and political point of view, standards promise a quick and efficient way to identify and rectify what is wrong with schools, teachers, and higher education. After all, educators have been claiming to reform themselves for many decades with apparent limited success. The public seems fed up with endless cycles of educational improvement fads that have had little effect on student learning and school achievement. The appeal of standards is that they express simple, desirable statements of goals and outcomes. The use of standards is familiar and has proven to be an effective quality control strategy in other settings, including manufacturing, business, and the professions. Consumers clearly understand the meanings of a warranty, a guarantee, and a service contract. Professional standards imply similar commitments.

Herein lies the threat to educators. Teaching and learning are complex endeavors contingent on many factors outside the control of schools and educators. On one hand, research-based teaching practice does not automatically result in high student achievement. We know that student learning is to a degree a personal, constructive activity and can be strongly influenced by social and economic factors. On the other hand, recent, large-scale research studies suggest that teacher preparation, ability, and experience account for more variation in student achievement than any other school factor (Ferguson, 1991; Greenwald, Hedges, & Laine, 1996; Sanders & Rivers, 1996).

Many educators perceive standards to be another layer of state regulation to contend with. Such restrictions, in the minds of many teachers and school leaders, direct attention and resources away from their real mission of teaching children. Rather than spending time with children in the act of teaching, time is wasted generating narrow evidence of teaching or learning and inventing arguments to justify one's acts.

In addition, standards can be seen as a code word for standardization, which discounts variation in performance due to a number of reasons. Holding all students to high, rigorous standards, for example, can prevent children with special needs from succeeding. Gains made in accommodating diversity can quickly disappear if standards are narrowly interpreted. Other critics question the reliability of assessments that measure performance against standards, especially for so "loosely structured and dynamic" (Moss & Schutz, 1999) an activity as teaching.

Neither the public and political point of view nor the professional perspective identified above of the use of standards recognizes the real potential of the standards movement in education. Both perspectives oversimplify what standards are and how they can be used.

THE ROLE OF STANDARDS IN PROFESSIONALIZATION

Yinger (1999), drawing on Abbott's (1988) sociological analysis of the professionalization process, has argued that educational standards is one of the most powerful tools available for professionalizing teaching. By depicting professionalization as a process of claiming and acquiring jurisdictional authority for defining, thinking about, and acting on specific problems of practice, Yinger's model highlights the role of abstract professional knowledge and its translation into internal professional social controls such as standards.

Professional knowledge, especially abstract and case knowledge, forms the basis for a profession's claim to cognitive jurisdiction. Cognitive jurisdiction, simply stated is the right to conceptualize, categorize, and act on professional problems. This right to conceptualize, categorize, and take action can be claimed when professionals demonstrate mastery of a body of abstract knowledge. This abstract knowledge base is generated and legitimized primarily by the academy. The formal rationality embodied in the academic disciplines and academic professional study provides culturally accepted formulations of the world of practice and, through the knowledge base, can

ROBERT J. YINGER and MARTHA S. HENDRICKS-LEE   97

generate new practice. The knowledge base also generates and legitimizes the establishment of standards for the profession. These standards establish internal control by the profession over training, entry to practice, and practice itself. By doing so, the profession consolidates its legitimacy and jurisdiction by demonstrating attention to performance and quality control.

Although knowledge is sufficient for establishing cultural and cognitive jurisdiction, a profession has to interact with and claim social jurisdiction in the arenas of public opinion, the legal system, and organizational systems. In other words, a large part of becoming a profession involves convincing the rest of society of the legitimacy of that status. This is especially true in the way the public, legal, and organizational arenas endorse the establishment of standards for professional training, licensure, and ethical practice. In claiming social jurisdiction, a profession asks society to recognize its cognitive structure through exclusive rights; jurisdiction has not only a cultural formulation but a social structure as well.

Standards play a dual role in the development of professions. First, standards become a major way to demonstrate to the public and to policy makers that the profession has sufficient quality controls for the processes of professional education, for controlling entry to the profession (i.e., licensure or certification), and for basing effective practice on a defensible knowledge base. Standards, in other words, can be used by professionals to improve the quality of practice and at the same time gain social and cultural recognition and legitimization.

Second, standards function as parameters and guidelines for conducting professional work. They can define effective practice in terms of desired outcomes and in terms of preferred procedures and performance. Standards can prescribe the inquiry frameworks that are used for assessing and creating new knowledge and practice. Standards also can become the basis for establishing training and continuing education parameters.

THE ROLE OF STANDARDS IN IMPROVING
AND EMPOWERING PRACTICE

The current movement toward standards for teachers began as a response to the harsh criticism of education in the early 1980s. The Carnegie Forum on Education and the Economy (1986) aimed to remedy the dire state of American education described in *A Nation at Risk* (National Commission on Excellence in Education, 1983) by proposing high and rigorous standards for teachers (i.e., *A Nation Prepared: Teachers for the 21st Century*). In 1987, the National Board of Professional Teaching Standards (NBPTS) was established to identify, describe, and provide assessment parameters for accomplished teaching. Also in 1987, the Council of Chief State School Officers sponsored the formation of the Interstate New Teacher Assessment and Support Consortium (INTASC) to facilitate collaboration among states engaged in rethinking initial teacher certification and licensure. A year earlier, the Holmes Group, a consortium of nearly 100 research universities involved in teacher education, was established to address concerns about the quality of teacher education and development. The recommendations of the Holmes Group in *Tomorrow's Teachers* (1986) called for standards-based accreditation of teacher education.

By the mid 1990s, the work of each of these groups revealed a growing consensus nationally about what teachers should know and be able to do. Expectations for teacher knowledge and performance were identified and aligned to form a coherent and consistent continuum for teacher development from preservice preparation, including the design of teacher education programs, through advanced certification. It is worth noting that these groups that have been most active in defining the profession through standards constitute the profession itself. Teachers, teacher educators, school administrators, and other professional organizations, including teacher unions, have participated in the creation of the standards and in setting the accountability measures. The widespread support of these standards, for example, by the National Commission on Teaching & America's Future, comes from the teaching profession itself as well as from governmental and philanthropic organizations.

The formulations of professional standards developed in the past 10 years have taken a different approach and form than the teacher accountability movements of the 1960s and 1970s. Rather than describing teaching ability as a set of specific behavioral competencies, standards are written as broad statements that address teacher knowledge and skill. For example, NBPTS (1994) has identified five core propositions from which the standards for certification areas arise. The third proposition is stated as follows:

Teachers are responsible for managing and monitoring student learning. National Board certified teachers create settings that sustain the interest of their students. They command a range of instructional techniques and know when each is appropriate. They know how to motivate and engage groups of students. They use multiple methods for measuring student growth and can clearly explain student performance to parents.

Similarly, INTASC has articulated 10 principles undergirding their standards. The 5th INTASC principle states, "The teacher uses an understanding of individual and group motivation and behavior to create a learning environment that encourages positive social interaction, active engagement in learning, and self-motivation." These examples reveal the abstract, decontextualized, almost inarguable nature of standards. Standards, in and of themselves, are broad and benign. It is in the use of standards that conflicts and tensions arise.

INTERNAL AND EXTERNAL ACCOUNTABILITY

Our own experiences in teacher education reform provide examples of how standards can be a powerful tool for teaching, learning, reflection, and professional development—not only for novice and experienced teachers but also for university faculty. In 1986, the University of Cincinnati College of Education decided to heed the national calls for educational reform and redesign its teacher education program. Rather than beginning the design process by focusing on curricular changes, the faculty from all departments in the College of Education, interested faculty from the College of Arts and Sciences, and public school teachers and administrators met to discuss basic questions about teaching: What does it mean to be a well-educated teacher? What is effective teaching? What kinds of knowledge and skill are needed for effective practice? These discussions occurred over a 2-year period and resulted in a document, *A Pattern Language for Teaching* (College of Education, University of Cincinnati, 1987, 1993, 1998). The *Pattern Language* proved to be a vehicle for record keeping, place holding, and for documenting a hard-won consensus among faculty and across departmental and college lines about the critical issues of teaching and learning. The *Pattern Language*, ranging from 130 to 98 individual patterns in its various iterations, is organized into three tiers:

1. College core patterns represent the overall mission and goals of teacher education. The patterns are study and practice of teaching and learning, multicultural focus, individual diversity, urban mission, inquiry and reflection, leadership in education, inclusive learning community, professional development, and lifelong learning.
2. Outcomes identify the knowledge, skills, and dispositions our students are expected to incorporate into their teaching repertoires.
3. Professional study and professional practice patterns name the activities and structures through which students acquire and learn to effectively use the outcome patterns. The study patterns provide knowledge and skills, and the practice patterns provide the context and situations within which to craft the knowledge and skills.

Although not fully cognizant of it at the time, we were creating a set of knowledge-based standards on which to build our new programs. Framed as a language, the knowledge base had the flexibility necessary for all age levels and content areas, the inventiveness and creativity to be functional in multiple contexts, and the improvisational nature to guide varying levels of skill and knowledge. In essence, we had developed a language of practice for teaching that was codified and communicative (Yinger, 1987). Meanings in this language had been communally negotiated and adopted. Built into the *Pattern Language* concept was the commitment to revisit the language to ensure its viability and practicality and to check for communal comprehension. The three publication dates, listed above, indicate the revisions.

The redesigned teacher education programs and each individual course arose from the *Pattern Language*. Just as the language was developed communally, courses were developed across departments and programs. Confusion, conflicting interpretations, and disagreements about content were immediately apparent. For example, in the development of Human Learning, an educational foundations course that was to be coordinated with a secondary education course called Curriculum Decision Making, faculty disagreed about the meaning and applications of constructivism. The widespread discussions constructing the standards allowed the disagreement to surface in the first place. The resolution—to present the competing definitions and arguments in support of both as course content—was possible only because faculty had learned to negotiate the standards.

In addition to providing the stimulus for articulation of professional education, the *Pattern Language* acted as a means of internal accountability. Professional programs were no longer the business of particular faculty but became the concern of the entire college. The *Pattern Language* provided the mechanisms for widespread assessment of programs. If a program as a whole did not incorporate all of the patterns, then the program was deemed lacking and the omissions were clear. The content and goals of every course were known to all and available for inspection. No longer were courses left to individual faculty discretion; the programs were clearly articulated and integrated so that success in one area was dependent on success in another.

The *Pattern Language* proved invaluable as a means of external accountability as well. The well-defined knowledge, skills, and dispositions and the structures and activities through which these would be acquired enabled the College of Education to make commitments about the quality of its graduates long before students enrolled in the programs. The magnitude of the redesign process, as indicated in the *Pattern Language*, provided the argument for the financial support of the university administration. In the early days of our partnership with Cincinnati Public Schools (CPS) and the Cincinnati

Federation of Teachers (CFT), when a joint committee explored the creation of professional practice schools, the *Pattern Language* and the commitments to quality to which it attested provided enough assurance that the CFT contributed 50 teaching positions (and the allocated salaries) to establish part-time, load-bearing, paid internships for teacher education students.

FROM KNOWLEDGE BASE TO PERFORMANCE STANDARDS

Although the *Pattern Language* proved invaluable in developing shared understandings, in articulating conceptual frameworks, and specifying commitments to quality, it was too unwieldy to present to students directly or to use for the evaluation of student performance. Each program, then, collapsed and embedded the knowledge base into performance standards that were also linked to emerging Ohio beginning teacher standards informed by INTASC and NBPTS standards.

Secondary education, the example used throughout this article, formed a committee of schoolteachers and professors who identified eight themes (learning, instruction, content, curriculum, context, professional growth and development, grounded theory and knowledge, and collaboration) into which the outcome patterns fit. The committee wrote rubrics to define and specify the range of performance indicators. These themes formed the basis of all course and practica objectives and goals, feedback, and assessment provided to the secondary education students. The act of developing defensible performance assessments—and, more important in our experience, in calibrating the assessment instrument—caused schoolteachers and university faculty to reflect on and assess their own performance in the classroom. Can, for example, an intern perform in an "exemplary" manner within the parameters identified for "learning"? Should the ratings be used solely to describe the performance for beginning teachers, or would a more informative and effective use of the rubrics be in describing the performance of experienced teachers? If the latter, then interns would understand their teaching practice in relation to expectations for professional teaching.

Reading through our standards, or the INTASC's or NBPTS's, the language is so abstract and benign as to be almost meaningless. The exemplary rating for our standard concerning learning (i.e., from the rubric from our Intern Assessment Instrument) includes the following language:

The intern consistently aids learners' processing of new information into their present system of knowledge and to make connections with their own lives. The intern consistently demonstrates that he/she understands the complexity of learning and the high-level processes used to acquire learning.

Although no one would disagree that this is an indicator of accomplished teaching, identifying aspects of one's practice that match the indicator can be a matter of some debate. To make the standards effective for discussing and assessing teaching, faculty members use the standards from Day 1 of the preparation program. Early written assignments are graded and the grades justified in terms of the work's approach toward the standard. Both school-teachers and university faculty testify to the impact using the standards has had on their own teaching and learning. Expectations for student work (public school student or teacher preparation student) are presented more clearly, and feedback is precise. Assessments are supported with evidence, and suggestions for improvement are phrased in standards language.

Initially, students resist such assessment and feedback. They appear more comfortable with decontextualized judgments. Eventually, however, the students learn to speak the language and see their practice in relation to the standards. By the end of their internship year, we believe they have a rich understanding of teaching and learning, one that would be difficult to achieve without a standards-based program.

As discussed above, our preparation programs require a half-time, year-long internship in which interns have full responsibility for classroom teaching in CPS. CPS is like many large, urban districts, with high poverty rates, high dropout rates, and low student achievement on statewide standardized tests. Despite course work and practica geared toward urban environments, many of our interns, often from suburban homes, do not feel prepared to teach urban students at the beginning of their internships. As one of our teacher mentors states, "Our kids are very open, loud, aggressive and confrontational— these kids are all the things that the intern is not" (Keiffer-Barone, 1998, p. 147). A common refrain from the interns initially is, "I want some one to tell me what to do with these kids."

In our old programs, traditionally structured and not informed by the use of standards, a cooperating teacher or university supervisor likely would reply to the student teacher's request with a directive, "Try this or try doing that." Although such a response might be grounded in theory or the wisdom of practice, the novice teacher has no way of knowing what professional knowledge, if any, is prompting the recommended action. The advice, then, is more idiosyncratic than professional and does nothing to assist the novice in developing a repertoire of teaching strategies. Learning to use standards and speak the language of standards prevents this situation from occurring.

Being conversant in standards means framing all activities and events in terms of educational issues. The problem is not with "these kids" but must be couched in one of the eight standards in the secondary education program. For the interns, especially in the first months of teaching, the most appropriate standard with which to characterize the difficulties they experience is "context." Most of them are not familiar and have had little experience with the cultural, socioeconomic, and ethnic backgrounds of the CPS students; the norms of large, urban high schools; and the expectations of the particular high school in which they are working. Seeing the problem as one of context places the onus on the intern to learn more about the students and the urban environment. As a mentor teacher explains to his interns,

Wait until you call home and you'll find out why that is, because conversations are going like crazy on the other end of the phone and you're like—this is chaos. No, it's not chaos; it's perfectly organized. If things were any other way, it would be strange and unnatural to them. It's a different kind of standard. And there are times when one is appropriate and another's appropriate, but that doesn't make it bad. (Keiffer-Barone, 1998, p. 123)

Placing the apparent "chaos" in relation to the teaching standard addressing context links the situation to an educational issue—effective teaching and learning must include the contexts of the students. The novice teacher's task becomes one of professional development: to learn the cultural, ethnic, and/or communicative norms of the students. Again, the mentor teacher advises,

To deal with [our students], you have to be their way a little more. Learn that your style is not the best style. Even though some of their behavior is not acceptable at all, it isn't horrible to them. It just needs to be channeled and used correctly. Assuming your cultural values are the right ones would be a mistake. (Keiffer-Barone, 1998, p. 147)

Essentially, the mentor is encouraging the novice teachers to negotiate the norms of the classroom with the students. Such advice, of course, runs counter to conventional wisdom, which instructs new teachers to maintain tight control in the classroom and ease up as the year progresses. The image set by the standard and reinforced by its contextualization in actual experience is that teaching and learning are complex activities, requiring continuous negotiation on several levels, not the least of which are communicative and behavioral patterns.

It is interesting to note our data show that later in the year, once the interns have recovered from their "culture shock," issues of student diversity and learning difficulties are cast in the standard addressing *instruction*. Instruction is defined by our *Secondary Education Program Handbook* as

the design, construction, and adjustment of environments and activities aimed at the achievement of specific outcomes by learners. . . . A teacher's decisions about instruction and the management of classrooms and students are based upon an understanding of the content to be taught and the learning processes of the students. Furthermore, effective teachers find a best fit between their instructional repertoire and the needs of the moment.

By this time, the beginning teachers know their students, and impasses to student learning often are characterized in terms of limited instructional strategies. As one intern stated, "There are so many good kids in this class . . . I need to try another strategy" (Keiffer-Barone, 1998, p. 176).

LEARNING TO WORK WITH STANDARDS

The above example illustrates the value of standards for creating a discourse to name and reflect on classroom interaction. That the interns initially interpret the challenges of teaching in terms of learning to negotiate the classroom context and later in terms of limited instructional repertoire suggests many important features about standards. First, good performance standards always place the teacher in relation to the students and activities of the classroom. Although the interns do have to develop their own teaching styles, this development is not simply dependent on their personal characteristics but is in relation to the students they teach and the expectations of the profession. Again, teaching is not regarded as an idiosyncratic activity to which some are born and some are not; rather, teaching requires continuous learning and mastery of knowledge and skills.

Second, taking teaching and learning standards seriously forces the teacher to interpret classroom interaction "in terms of"; that is, standards present a conceptual framework and a language that must be rectified to classroom life. Research-based standards are not easily dismissed; argument and evidence become a necessary part of the professional teacher's repertoire. Knowledge and thought become more explicit in a standards-based environment, which provides a platform for reflection, discourse, and improvement among novices and experienced practitioners.

Effective use of standards requires considerable knowledge about the immediate pedagogical situation to which they are applied. Relevant features of the situation are placed within the parameters set by the standard. Throughout the internship year, the standards assist interns and mentors in understanding classroom teaching and learning; often, they are used to identify or diagnose areas that need improvement. At the end of the year, however, the interns construct portfolios, which demonstrate their understanding of the standards and present arguments that they have mastered the standards. In the portfolio, interns show how their pedagogical knowledge has developed both in narrative and by including artifacts from the year, such as lesson plans, student work, and reflective writing. Their task is to interpret the standards in terms of their preparation program and pedagogical knowledge, to interpret their teaching in terms of the standards, and to argue that they, in fact, have met the standards by providing evidence and explaining its significance.

CONCLUSION

Because of the timing of and the strategy used by the College of Education in our redesign of teacher education, our work with standards has been the reverse of most other institutions. We developed a knowledge base and a set of standards as an internal mechanism for consistency, coherence, and accountability. *The Knowledge Base for the Beginning Teacher*, sponsored by the American Association of Colleges of Teacher Education (Reynolds, 1989), was published at the same time that we were developing our *Pattern Language*. The development of the program themes also was concurrent with the development of standards by the INTASC and NBPTS. Our task, then, has been to translate our internal standards into the nationally recognized standards and map local, institutional commitments on to what the profession as a whole values and expects of its members. For most people, the reverse process is in order. Institutions, both schools and higher education, must internalize the standards put forth statewide and nationally. Teacher educators and practitioners must learn to conceive of, learn to speak in, and learn to assess their work in terms of emerging standards. Doing so will develop the cognitive and social jurisdiction for teaching mentioned earlier. More important, standards-based teacher preparation and professional development will continue the documented trend of better teachers and teaching promoting higher student learning and achievement.

REFERENCES

Abbott, A. D. (1988). *The system of professions: An essay on the division of expert labor.* Chicago: University of Chicago Press.
Carnegie Forum on Education and the Economy, Task Force on Teaching as a Profession. (1986). *A nation prepared: Teachers for the 21st century.* New York: Author.
College of Education, University of Cincinnati. (1987). *A pattern language for teaching.* Cincinnati, OH: Author.

College of Education, University of Cincinnati. (1993). *A pattern language for teaching*. Cin--cinnati, OH: Author.

College of Education, University of Cincinnati. (1998). *A pattern language for teaching*. Cincinnati, OH: Author.

Ferguson, R. F. (1991). Paying for public education: New evidence of how and why money matters. *Harvard Journal on Legislation, 28,* 465-498.

Greenwald, R. L., Hedges, L.V., & Laine, R. D. (1996). The effect of school resources on student achievement. *Review of Educational Research, 66,* 361-396.

The Holmes Group. (1986). *Tomorrow's teachers*. East Lansing, MI: Author.

Keiffer-Barone, S. (1998). *Why they bail: The ecology of intern attrition in a professional development school*. Unpublished doctoral dissertation, University of Cincinnati.

Moss, P. A., & Schutz, A. (1999). Risking frankness in educational assessment. *Phi Delta Kappan, 80,* 668-695.

National Board of Professional Teaching Standards. (1994). *What teachers should know and be able to do*. Detroit, MI: Author.

National Commission on Excellence in Education. (1983). *A nation at risk: The imperative for educational reform*. Washington, DC: Author.

Reynolds, M. C. (Ed.). (1989). *Knowledge base for the beginning teacher*. New York: Pergamon.

Sanders, W. L., & Rivers, J. C. (1996). *Cumulative and residual effects of teachers on future student academic achievement*. Knoxville: University of Tennessee Press.

Yinger, R. J. (1987). Learning the language of practice. *Curriculum Inquiry, 17,* 293-318.

Yinger, R. J. (1999). The role of standards in teaching and teacher education. In G. A. Griffin (Ed.), *The education of teachers. Ninety-eighth yearbook of the National Society for the Study of Education*. Chicago: National Society for the Study of Education.

Balancing the Politics of Two Cultures: Cincinnati Initiative for Teacher Education and the Cincinnati Professional Practice Schools Partnership

ARLENE HARRIS MITCHELL,
LOUIS A. CASTENELL, JR.,
MARTHA S. HENDRICKS-LEE,
and TOM MOONEY

The Cincinnati Initiative for Teacher Education (CITE) and the development of the Cincinnati Professional Practice Schools formulated a partnership among the University of Cincinnati, the Cincinnati Public School District, and the Cincinnati Federation of Teachers. The success of this venture has been achieved through the recognition of the different institutional cultures. The political factors of faculty roles, accountability, and funding are discussed in the article while giving a brief historical background of the conception, planning, and execution of this successful collaboration.

THE PURPOSE OF this article is to tell the story of the Cincinnati Initiative for Teacher Education (CITE) and the development of the Cincinnati Professional Practice Schools Partnership, a collaboration among the University of Cincinnati, Cincinnati Public Schools (CPS), and the Cincinnati Federation of Teachers (CFT). Much of the success of the partnership can be attributed to its leadership. Persons in leadership roles throughout the 10-year history of the partnership developed strategies that were successful in engaging various

EDUCATIONAL POLICY, Vol. 14 No. 1, January and March 2000 107-119
© 2000 Corwin Press, Inc.

power brokers and constituents in the goals of the partnership. The key to developing the different strategies for the different spheres of power lies in recognizing the cultures of each. In this article, we will analyze the politics that have been successfully navigated to achieve the approval, resources, and actual work required to pull off such an endeavor. The actual story of "how we did it" will be used to illustrate our assertions about leadership and political strategizing.

Although we believe that successful systemic reform can occur at any time, context played a pivotal role in our success. In the early 1980s, the educational system in the United States came under harsh criticism, with reports such as *A Nation at Risk* (National Commission on Excellence in Education, 1983) claiming that we, in effect, had been committing an act of unthinking, unilateral, educational disarmament (p. 5). Two responses to these criticisms laid the groundwork for the Cincinnati Professional Practice School Partnership, one that greatly influenced the university and one that greatly influenced the teachers and schools. For this article, we first discuss the impact of the partnership on the university. Then, we chronicle the history of the partnership in the schools and with the union.

THE UNIVERSITY

William Bergquist's *The Four Cultures of the Academy* (1992) captures the complexity of higher education. He speaks specifically to understanding cultural dynamics of academic institutions and how these concepts must be understood before effective organizational improvement can occur. The four cultures are collegial, managerial, developmental, and negotiating. Briefly, collegial culture can be associated with norms found within disciplines and the core values of research and scholarship, managerial culture seeks meaning in academic organization and accountability, developmental culture is concerned with professional development and new initiatives, and negotiating culture lies in the establishment of equitable and egalitarian policies and procedures. In Cincinnati, those in College of Education leadership positions used their knowledge of these cultures to orchestrate a reform effort that was both "top down" and "bottom up." Without the support of the university administration and without the participation of the faculty, systemic reform would not have been possible. The extent to which these cultures are used to reinforce systemic change suggests the probability for successful transformation.

In 1983, 17 education deans from large, comprehensive research universities with teacher training programs met to discuss the low quality of teacher education in the United States. These deans became known as the Holmes

Group. Soon thereafter, an expanded group of scholars from well-respected universities wrote, and the Holmes Group published, *Tomorrow's Teachers* (1986), which identified standards of quality for teacher education and the teaching profession. The University of Cincinnati joined the Holmes Group in 1986. Note that the university, not the college, joined. This requirement of the Holmes Group had two positive consequences for us. The first played on the culture of *collegiality* nationally; the original members of the Holmes Group were select, and an invitation to become a colleague in this group was prestigious. The invitation indicated our status as a member of those analyzing and deciding the core values for professional education. Second, joining the Holmes Group set up a more collegial culture between the College of Education and the university administration. It established common interests and more specific purposes, something colleges of education, as opposed to colleges of medicine or engineering, do not usually enjoy. Questions were asked about why an initiative to improve teacher education should merit favorable support when other academic units were in need of augmentation. This collegial culture required us to draw on the recommendations and policy statements of numerous professional disciplines and organizations.

Being recognized as a part of a national movement satisfied the university administration initially and allowed the college leadership to focus its energy on the College of Education and its faculty. During the next 2 years after joining the Holmes Group, an interesting mix of the developmental and managerial cultures came into play in the college. Initially, the conditions for a developmental culture were stressed. A task force was appointed and charged with developing a conceptual framework for reform. College faculty, then, initially agreed to a design process rather than to particular structural or curricular changes. The process emphasized participation, local control, piecemeal growth, and organic order. In other words, the agree-on process allowed plenty of opportunity for thought, conversation, and deliberation from everyone involved in teacher education. By first promoting the developmental culture, which features new initiatives and professional growth, we were able to establish the ground rules and procedures. These ground rules guaranteed that growth and professional development would not be imposed on us but would be decided on and engaged in by us.

Although college leadership supported the developmental culture, the actual work of the faculty was to rethink and redesign a managerial culture. College faculty quite literally sought to develop a new meaning of professional teacher education. To do this, we had to reconceptualize everyone's roles in the endeavor, establish common understanding, and develop new means of accountability. Therefore, much of the early work of the redesign process was spent in conversation. Like many colleges in universities across the country, education had become too departmentalized, with the faculty in one program rarely meeting faculty in other programs to discuss educational issues. This was particularly true across divisional lines, where, for example, educational foundations faculty never had occasion to meet with teacher education faculty. Basic questions about the nature of teaching and learning were discussed by faculty from all programs in the college, and consensus was reached. As part of the agreed-on design process, negotiations and agreement were documented in the *Pattern Language* (College of Education, University of Cincinnati, 1987, 1993, 1998), a collaboratively developed language of practice. Entries into the *Pattern Language* included a rationale based in research or the wisdom, a prescriptive statement, and a list of indicators that would provide evidence of pattern enactment. Entries into the language also acted as placeholders for such conceptions as professional development schools, master teachers, and school-based faculty, conceptions critical to program design but dependent on the contributions of future partners.

The language, which became the National Council for Accreditation of Teacher Education (NCATE)–approved knowledge base and conceptual framework in 1993, was organized hierarchically. The first nine entries in the 1998 revised version (earlier iterations had 10) are called College Core Patterns, which embody the overall mission and goals for teacher education in the college. Although the College Core Patterns frame the nature of professional programs, the next grouping of patterns, Ways of Knowing, Ways of Doing, and Ways of Being, are more specific and are considered outcomes for student achievement. These patterns highlight some of the individual components of teaching expertise identified by research, theory, and the wisdom of practice, and they are likely to be expressed in complex combinations in student learning experiences. The remainder of the language is organized into Professional Studies and Professional Practice, and each category identifies the activities and structures through which the college core and the outcomes are realized.

By first identifying, and then coming to consensus on, crucial factors in the preparation of teachers, the college designed articulated, integrated teacher education programs. All courses and experiences clearly identified the knowledge, skills, and dispositions students were to acquire; and the courses comprising programs included all agreed-on components. Initially, all teacher education programs were dual degree (a bachelor's in arts and sciences to ensure depth and breadth of content area knowledge and a bachelor's in education), an extended professional component with graduate-level study, and a yearlong internship. Special education was designed to be a master's program with an entrance requirement of a certificate in regular education. (Due to the change from teacher certification to teacher licensure in the state of Ohio, CITE programs are evolving, and some programs no longer require dual degrees, although the commitment to in-depth, upperlevel study in content areas remains.)

Although college faculty members were busy designing and developing new programs, the leadership needed to continue to persuade university administration that the endeavor was worthy, especially in light of its cost. As suggested above, part of the task was to stress the collegial culture, in which the University of Cincinnati was becoming a national player. An external review of the developing teacher education programs by well-known educational experts proved convincing. Without national endorsements and support, the scope of our programs would have been minimized.

During these years, faculty members raised questions about their existing responsibilities, especially as they related to teaching loads and advising. As a result, we needed to review our entire managerial culture. We needed to guarantee that a legitimate enrollment management process was in place, and we needed to ensure fiscal prudence. To allay some faculty concerns about the loss of faculty time, we established a student-advising center.

Next, we had to explain how this initiative would enhance professional development. This *developmental* culture called for us to show how the interlocking professional development of faculty is tied to the simultaneous professional development of teachers. We eventually set aside professional development funds to provide incentives for all parties to ensure continuous improvements. Some of the activities we sponsored include team teaching, paper presentations at regional and national conferences, research projects, joint participation in policy formation in professional teacher education organizations, and pursuing external funds to expand our work.

Finally, we were asked to vote on these sweeping changes before approval would be granted. We thus had a series of faculty meetings that at times were contentious. Issues debated included faculty workload, institutional rewards such as tenure and promotion, and the boundaries of the proposed partnership. This *negotiating* culture required us to reach agreement; otherwise, the university would not support this initiative regardless of its merit. Successfully navigating these turbulent waterways was the only way to create the time and resources for our partnership.

THE SCHOOL DISTRICT AND THE UNION

Although the college was examining its efforts toward providing professional quality education, CPS and CFT formed a partnership for the professionalization of teaching. Professionalization was of national concern to the American Federation of Teachers (AFT), in part because of a need to convince the tax-paying public that school personnel and unions were dedicated to more than pay raises and benefits increases. A 17-day strike in 1977 and intense negotiations had raised teachers' salaries in CPS, and broader issues of urban schooling became the grounds for a long-lasting partnership between the district and the union. As with the university, the school district and the union felt compelled to respond to the critics of education in the early 1980s.

Despite a context conducive to examining education and making changes, the partnership between CPS and CFT was not easily established. Preparing for negotiating the 1985 collective bargaining agreement marked a change in union leadership strategies. Much of the gains teachers had made in the past were due to militancy, but our new strategy focused on communication. First, we surveyed the membership and clearly established the professionalization as our primary goal. Teacher preference indicated that the many factors that influence the quality of education were more important to them than an increase in salary. This survey provided the factual basis for skilled communication. We mounted a massive campaign called "Bargaining for Better Schools," which presented improved education as the union's primary negotiating goal. Within the CFT's concept of improved education was limits on class size. Typically, limits on class size are considered working conditions, a standard area of negotiation in a labor contract. However, we framed the issue as one of educational quality, which, of course, it is. This campaign, which included newspaper ads, radio spots, and opportunities for parental and community input, positioned the CFT as an advocate for students, parents, and community members, in addition to being an advocate for teachers.

One outcome of the 1985 teacher contract was implementation of the Peer Assistance and Appraisal Program, a program in which experienced teachers are in charge of mentoring and appraising teachers new to the district and in which experienced teachers help teachers identified as having performance problems. Furthermore, a commitment to implementing a career ladder that acknowledged differences in teachers' experience and skill with opportunities for new kinds of work and for increased salaries was established.

The 1988 *Collective Bargaining Agreement* (Cincinnati Board of Education and the CFT, 1988) was negotiated using a "win-win" or "principled" negotiations process based on methods developed at the Harvard Negotiation Project (Fisher & Ury, 1981). The team members were trained extensively by Conflict Management, Inc., which also facilitated the process. The success of the method is clear in the contract, which has a preface explaining new, mutual commitments, along with an addendum, a trust agreement, and joint recommendations—good ideas generated during the process that both sides wanted preserved.

This contract made provisions for the development and implementation of the Career in Teaching program, a commitment of both the union and the board to improving teaching:

A profession offers opportunities for professional growth, involvement in decision making, communication and collaboration and increased responsibilities and accountability. By implementing change in the organization of schools, teachers will have the opportunity to take on greater responsibilities which will bring with it greater status, higher salary, opportunities to collaborate, as well as leadership roles to improve instruction and student achievement. (Cincinnati Board of Education and the CFT, 1988, p. 13)

Of most importance for this article, the trust agreement specified strategies for the recruitment and training of teachers:

If we agree to pursue the development of one or more professional practice schools, we would seek funding for planning and development, determine the resources needed to operate such a school, and investigate how these resources can be funded. We might explore with local colleges and universities what assistance they might provide and role professional practice schools could play in teacher training and certification. Increasing collaboration with the nearby post-secondary institutions was a goal of the Board's Long Range Plan. (Cincinnati Board of Education and the CFT, 1988, p. 1)

In April 1987, Tom Mooney, the president of the CFT, was invited to serve on a task force of the AFT to explore the concept of a professional practice school (PPS), a school with the tri-fold goals of (a) supporting student success, (b) inducting beginning teachers and providing professional development of experienced teachers, and (c) supporting systematic inquiry directed toward the improvement of practice. Initially, the AFT Task Force members feared that dealing with three missions would prove overwhelming, but they came to believe that the three missions are inextricably intertwined. The AFT analyses and descriptions of the changes in the professions and the structures needed to support these changes were published in *Professional Practice Schools: Building a Model, Volumes I and II* (AFT, 1988, 1990). In fact, Mooney wrote a position paper describing a vision for teacher education in terms that were quite similar to University of Cincinnati's eventual design, featuring a content area degree and an extended, paid teaching internship modeled after medical training.

Although there are vast differences between universities and schools, many of the leadership issues we face are the same. To achieve progress in educational reform, all of us relied on national findings and confirmation to justify and support our work. We had to persuade the external forces of the value of our work. And, leaders had to create internal support, leadership, and momentum within our constituencies.

CINCINNATI PROFESSIONAL PRACTICE SCHOOL PARTNERSHIP

Although historically school personnel had served on university committees and university personnel on school committees, neither partner knew the scope of the work of the other. In 1990, the first formal work among the partners specifically for the purpose of developing PPSs began. A joint planning committee with five members from each of the partners met for a year to identify a cost model, application process, and design parameters. This design strategy modeled the success CPS and CFT had experienced previously and ensured institutional commitments from all partners. At the time of initial discussions, the district was hiring 200 to 300 beginning teachers per year. Because of the union's and the district's commitment to professionalization, which included participation in the training and induction of new teachers, CPS and CFT agreed to designate a maximum of 50 teaching positions as intern positions over an extended implementation period. More specifically, when a teacher vacancy became available in a PPS, the position would be identified as an intern position, and the salary line contributed to intern pay. With a membership of more than 3,500 teachers, 50 positions amounted to reserving a little more than 1% for interns. The logic underlying the decision was simple: Rather than hiring a large number of beginning teachers whose preparation might or might not equip them to be successful in a large urban district, it is preferable to hire interns, whose training is known, and place them in situations that give them every opportunity to succeed.

The joint planning committee also developed a process for becoming a PPS. A request for proposal (RFP) to become a PPS was distributed to all schools in the district. The proposal asked schools—all teachers and administrators in a building—to work collaboratively to gauge potential success. The RFP required schools to describe the process used to build consensus and to write the application to become a PPS as well as to provide evidence of collaborative reform efforts undertaken in their building in the past. Whole school commitment, rather than departmental or individual commitments, is required, and expectations for participation are long term.

The Career in Teaching program, implemented in 1989 and discussed earlier, provided the teacher leadership necessary for the yearlong, load-bearing internship. As part of this program, new lead teacher positions were created: PPS coordinator, responsible for working with the teacher education programs and for building activities; and lead teacher mentor, responsible for the professional team at the school level. PPS lead teachers receive stipends, the cost of which the university and district split, and half-time release from classroom teaching. The lead teacher mentor has primary responsibility for coaching and mentoring the three to four interns on the team and collaborates with the career teacher mentors. Career teacher mentors on the professional team carry a full instructional load and have some supervisory responsibilities for the interns; for this service, career teacher mentors receive a supervisory stipend. Also on the team is a university faculty member. (In the early childhood education, secondary education, and special education program, each team has one university faculty member; in the elementary education program, one university faculty member serves the building.) The university faculty member also supports and mentors interns and represents and articulates the program design and activities. Coordination between intern teaching and university course work is facilitated through the university member.

In traditional student teaching models, the cooperating teacher provides supervision. Our partnership has developed the team model for a variety of reasons. First, the professional team provides a number of relationships to be established among the different members. The interns offer each other peer mentoring. The experienced teachers plan with the interns, observe and assess intern teaching, and assist with plans for improvement. Teams typically meet biweekly to share teaching strategies, materials, and methods; to discuss specific incidents or issues; and to promote and monitor student achievement. Teams also have responsibility for evaluating interns. Formal observations, assessments, and debriefing occur quarterly, although informal observations and conversations occur more frequently. Classroom teachers have a significant input into determining whether the interns are performing successfully.

The original intent was to pay interns half of a beginning teacher's salary for their half-time teaching. This plan allayed potential fears of reducing the unit cost of teachers and seeming to condone a cheaper way to cover classrooms. However, given the fluctuation of district funding cycles, this proved impossible. For example, for the first year that full internships (i.e., for students who had completed arts and sciences degrees and taken the newly designed professional courses) were implemented, the district made $32 million in budget cuts, laying off 120 teachers and offering early retirement to many others. The collective bargaining contract is clear that an intern will not replace a certified teacher; "any [intern] position within an area of certification subject to reduction in force shall be eliminated before a teacher within that area of certification is subject to reduction in force" (Cincinnati Board of Education and the CFT, 1985, p. 23). Therefore, all of the intern positions were relinquished (except in special education, which had no reduction in force). Currently, a pooling strategy is used in which all of the salary lines of identified positions are divided among the interns. The 1997 *Collective Bargaining Agreement* specifies salary ranges "up to 50%, but no less than 25% of the salary of a Class II teacher" (teacher with a bachelor's degree) (Cincinnati Board of Education and the CFT, 1997).

Perhaps most important, the design of PPS made possible the precise alignment necessary for systemic change. On one hand, the university and college are collaborating on a new way to improve and validate the work of the faculty. On the other, schools, the union, and the district adjusted their own labor agreement to embrace changes in our teacher education programs. These mutual events created a distinct culture, which spread accountability evenly among all partners. Newman, King, and Rigdon (1997) argued that strong internal accountability enhances organizational capacity. We witness daily a quiet revolution. For the first time, we have teachers and teacher educators collaborating on undergraduate curricula. We have teams of students, faculty, and teachers working on pedagogy, incredible exit interviews in which interns express strong confidence in their ability to teach, and emerging data that our recent graduates are experiencing success unlike other new teachers not exposed to the CITE model.

POLITICS OF FACULTY IN PARTNERSHIPS

As the two previous sections attest, each of the partners spent considerable time "putting our own house in order" before entering into the collaboration. Specifically, consensus was achieved about priorities and commitments. A vision of the profession of teaching was articulated by each of the partners, the strategies for attaining the visions were identified, and pathways begun. The vision for teaching as a profession was compatible but with each partner bringing different components. The analogy that we use is that of running the automobile and actually getting it to move. There are components that need to be in place for a car to move: the ignition, the steering wheel, the tires, the gas tank, and the engine, among others. If any one part of the machinery is not working, the car does not go. If the tires are flat but the ignition works, you will still not go very far and certainly not very fast. If there is no gas in the tank, again you are slowed to a stop. If the steering wheel is locked, you are in trouble. That is the way it is with the politics of partnerships. Partnerships work because each partner has a specialization that it brings to the partnership to make it whole. And, just as the key fits into the ignition to connect to the starter, collaboration is the key that makes a partnership successful.

But, each partner also has its external and internal cultures that are related to its specific institution, and that are not infused into the overall partnership. Faculty is a major element of a successful partnership. In the past, campus faculty was the only deciding factor on placements, on the interns' or student teachers' ability to manage a classroom, on what should be done in a classroom. In the new partnership, the classroom teacher is seen as an expert in what happens in a classroom. The classroom teacher is a very important asset to the acculturation of the intern and to the mentoring of the intern on a daily basis. In Cincinnati, each PPS has evolved in its own way, although common features persist. We have teams—which means that there may be three interns working with one or more teachers. In each model, we attempt to have a building coordinator who oversees the entire process within the building, as well as one or more faculty members involved with the school, with the teams, and with the interns. This type of collaboration helps to make for a successful internship that will lead to successful teachers.

To allow both school and campus faculty members to function, many things have to be taken into consideration. The role of the faculty members in their designated employment is important. That is, if they are classroom teachers, what are their other responsibilities in addition to or aside from mentoring and hosting interns? If they are campus faculty, what other time demands are placed on their instructional responsibilities, as well as research and service? When either faculty member is untenured, it imposes different types of problems. Putting new school faculty members into a situation in which, as they are developing as professionals, they face the added responsibility of being advocates for and models to the interns, is a major time commitment. To use untenured campus faculty in school situations in addition to or as even part of their instructional load when the tenure criteria have not been changed creates other kinds of problems that must be considered. Incorporated on each of these faculty members and on each institution is the reality of state and national accreditation bodies that are imposing standards to be met to better the teaching force.

It is important that the instructional partners develop the uniqueness of their roles. These roles must look different from the traditional roles of campus or school faculty. There must be some combination of the traditional roles to make a good collaborative relationship. It is important, however, that each maintains sight of the specialization and expertise that defines these traditional roles to make a comprehensive, coherent, and friendly partnership arrangement. For example, in the Cincinnati model, coordinators and classroom teachers are given opportunities to teach on campus in teacher preparation courses. It is important that they either carry a course or coteach a course.

More important, however, may be their contribution to the content of the course.

Politically there are also issues. The university is very clear about terminal degrees and the teaching of graduate-level courses. And, many practicing school faculty members do not carry this degree. At the same time, it is often requested that campus faculty model teaching, give input, or provide professional development to school faculty. Although this is an area that most campus faculty enjoy, the time to do it is often not a part of their schedule or it does not fit into the present tenure and promotion agenda of the university. But even here, we should avoid the old stereotype: Classroom teachers should be partners on campus as well. It is fair to say of the Cincinnati model that the input of schoolteachers has been infused directly into the structure of the teacher preparation program including content and facilitation. However, because of the culture and hierarchy of schools, this has not necessarily been reciprocated (but perhaps would be valuable) into the school environment. Politically, it must be remembered that faculty need the support of their institutions to be successful.

CONCLUSION

In short, we believe our success has been due to a number of aspects of the partnership. First, and perhaps the most important, is developing a vision that is broad enough to engage multiple constituents. Our vision became the professionalization of teaching, with a particular emphasis on professional education. The various constituents included in our partnership are the university central administration, faculty across colleges (especially the College of Arts and Sciences), and faculty in the College of Education, the Board of Education of Cincinnati Public Schools, CPS central administration, the bargaining unit (that, is all teachers in the district), and teachers and administrators in particular schools. The vision must be broad to incorporate the interests of all the constituents but cannot be diffuse. After all, institutional commitments and accountability measures must arise from the vision. To initiate and sustain such a partnership, leaders must be adept at "reading" the cultures of each constituent group and devising strategies that meet the expectations of these cultures. Such efforts secure the necessary time, space, and resources for those—in our case, the university and school faculties—who are actually doing the work.

REFERENCES

American Federation of Teachers. (1988). *Professional practice schools: Building a model* (Vol. 1). Washington, DC: Author.

American Federation of Teachers. (1990). *Professional practice schools: Building a model* (Vol. 2). Washington, DC: Author.

Bergquist, W. H. (1992). *The four cultures of the academy*. San Francisco: Jossey-Bass.

Cincinnati Board of Education and the Cincinnati Federation of Teachers. (1985). *Collective bargaining agreement*. Cincinnati, OH: Author.

Cincinnati Board of Education and the Cincinnati Federation of Teachers. (1988). *Collective bargaining agreement*. Cincinnati, OH: Author.

Cincinnati Board of Education and the Cincinnati Federation of Teachers. (1997). *Collective bargaining agreement*. Cincinnati, OH: Author.

College of Education, University of Cincinnati. (1987). *Pattern language for teaching*. Cincinnati, OH: Author.

College of Education, University of Cincinnati. (1993). *Pattern language for teaching*. Cincinnati, OH: Author.

College of Education, University of Cincinnati. (1998). *Pattern language for teaching*. Cincinnati, OH: Author.

Fisher, R., & Ury, W. (1981). *Getting to yes: Negotiating agreement without giving in*. Boston: Houghton Mifflin.

The Holmes Group. (1986). *Tomorrow's teachers*. East Lansing, MI: Author.

National Commission on Excellence in Education. (1983). *A nation at risk: The imperative for educational reform*. Washington, DC: Author.

Newman, F. M., King, M. B., & Rigdon, M. (1997). Accountability and school performance: Implications from restructuring schools. *Harvard Educational Review, 67*(1), 41-74.

Part 4

The Micropolitical Arena

Do Colleges of Liberal Arts and Sciences Need Schools of Education?

SALLY FROST MASON

The three central questions addressed in this article are the following: Whose responsibility is it to train teachers? What role should arts and sciences play in this process? And, do colleges of liberal arts and sciences need schools of education? Arguments are made for the value of collaboration across schools of education and colleges of arts and sciences and the roles that each of these groups can effectively play in education at all levels, from kindergarten through graduate school.

AS A LONGTIME faculty member and now administrator within the liberal arts and sciences sector of a Carnegie I research university, my attitudes and perceptions regarding the role that arts and sciences should play in teacher preparation have evolved over a 20-year period. My own discipline, biology, which I continue to teach at the introductory and more advanced levels, has provided me with direct opportunities to participate in teacher preparation, although, like so many of my colleagues, I was slow to realize the significance of the role I was playing. My intent in writing this article is to attempt to answer the following questions: Whose responsibility is it to train teachers? What role should arts and sciences play in this process? And, finally, do colleges of liberal arts and sciences need schools of education?

WHOSE RESPONSIBILITY IS IT TO TRAIN TEACHERS?

Faculty in the arts and sciences, like the general public, are quick to bemoan the sad state of public education in the United States today. The complaining often begins when their own children have been subjected to some

EDUCATIONAL POLICY, Vol. 14 No. 1, January and March 2000 121-128
© 2000 Corwin Press, Inc.

perceived shortcoming at the hands of a teacher in a local school. The problem is inevitably the teacher, and blame for the problem is attributed directly to schools of education. For those trained outside of a school of education, the mystification and, consequently, misperceptions of what actually occurs during teacher preparation are rampant and largely mythological. That these myths persist is promulgated by the attitudes of research faculty, especially those in the sciences, who believe that awarding of a Ph.D. automatically certifies one as a "teacher" despite the fact that no formal teacher training and, in some cases, no experience in teaching were required to complete the Ph.D.

Indeed, as I examine my own graduate training, the message from my mentors, professors, and peers was consistent. Research was the path to truly significant rewards; teaching was tolerated as the means to achieving lesser, but occasionally significant, rewards at universities. To spend great quantities of time in the preparation and delivery of college instruction often translates into doing so at the expense of research and consequently at the expense possibly of tenure. So, is it any wonder that arts and sciences faculty at research universities seem to have little regard for teaching, teachers, and schools of education?

Is the problem exclusively associated with large research universities? The answer to this question is a resounding no, because even small, private colleges with elite reputations in the liberal arts and sciences are currently attracting and hiring faculty who have been trained and indoctrinated at the larger, Ph.D.-granting research universities. These colleges are happy to attract research-trained faculty because they believe this will enhance their "research profile." The faculty are happy to relocate to the smaller school with the sometimes mistaken notion that they can devote more time to teaching and less to research. The reality is such that both the employer and employee in these cases may ultimately be disappointed. So, although my comments focus primarily on the personal experiences I have had at large research universities, I view this as a problem ubiquitous to higher education.

Although attitudes toward participation in K-16 opportunities by arts and sciences faculty are changing, movement has been slow and perhaps nonexistent in some sectors. I would argue that if teachers in public schools are ill prepared, it is more the fault of colleges of arts and sciences and the way we train Ph.D.s than it is the fault of schools of education. By placing so little value on teaching and devoting little effort to training Ph.D.s to teach, we send a curious message to our graduate students and faculty. In the sciences in particular, the "teaching" experience in graduate school often consists of assisting undergraduate students in a laboratory setting for which there is no lecture preparation, often no exam preparation, and even contact with students can be minimized if the laboratory exercises are clearly explained and relatively simple to conduct. This is a very different experience from walking into a classroom, perhaps with several hundred students, and lecturing for 60 to 80 minutes from lecture notes or an outline prepared in advance and with the expectation that you will discover a way to communicate this information effectively to the audience. The key phrase here is that you will "discover a way to communicate," because it is unlikely that if you were trained as a chemist or mathematician or physicist, for example, that you had ample room in your undergraduate or graduate curriculum for courses on effective communication. Indeed, when you discovered an effective and forceful lecturer in your own classroom experience, you likely were not challenged to determine why they were effective nor encouraged even to emulate them.

Is it any wonder that scientists and science faculty have been some of the most vocal critics of teacher preparation and schools of education? Ironically, it is within this subset of faculty that a significant portion of the blame may reside if we indeed believe that teachers are not trained well. Much of the vocal criticism of teacher education tends to focus on the lack of or poor training that teachers receive, especially in science and math. The aversion that school children may develop toward science and/or mathematics is frequently attributed directly to aversions that elementary schoolteachers themselves might have to these disciplines. And what is the source of such aversions?

Having debated at length with colleagues in the sciences about teaching philosophy and student learning, there continue to be attitudinal differences among faculty that clearly contribute to student aversion toward math and science. The instructor who is proud of achieving no better than a 50% average on an exam, who believes that only the top few percent of a given class can (or should be able to) truly master the concepts of their discipline, and who does little to change either his or her style or methods of teaching to improve learning and student performance contributes to this mythology. Even if one insists that such changes would seriously compromise the rigor and quality of a course, there are still ways to reduce student fears associated with science and math. Showing genuine interest in students and spending the time that it takes to reassure and work with them to demystify these subjects can go a long way to reversing attitudes without having to "dumb down" the curriculum. Designing and delivering a curriculum that is better suited to training a "scientifically educated" public rather than devoting efforts to training scientists and mathematicians almost exclusively is a more sound approach to reversing the negative attitudes and fears toward science and math. But in most universities, engaging in these activities will not lead to tenure and may not be recognized for any type of reward.

Although I have provided examples from within the sciences, I would not hesitate to add that similar transgressions exist within the humanities and social sciences faculty. I believe, however, that many faculty in these areas come to grasp the significance of the arts and sciences in teacher preparation more quickly than the scientists because they have often had a somewhat different experience in graduate school. Graduate students in these disciplines, prior to completion of their Ph.D.s, have often taught classes of their own, prepared lectures, and may have learned to love the classroom teaching experience as much as they love their research. This happens to science faculty as well, but for them, the realization of the role that teaching can play in higher education is acquired much more slowly if at all.

As a faculty member who had gained a passion relatively quickly for classroom teaching, imagine my horror on becoming an administrator to discover that the true value of teaching for some faculty was as "currency" to bargain away for more research time. This view is universally shared across all disciplines.

However, there is at last a growing acknowledgment in many departments at large universities (including science and math departments) that they bear a large share of the responsibility for training teachers. This has been helped in large measure by federal agencies, such as the National Science Foundation, and national consortial agencies, such as the American Association for the Advancement of Science, that are providing increasing opportunities for funding and collaborations between arts and sciences and education faculty (Bell & Buccino, 1997; CETP, 1998). So, too, are there now attempts to break the sacred boundaries of the faculty reward systems with Fund to Improve Post Secondary Education (FIPSE)–supported programs at several large universities designed to reexamine and change existing promotion and tenure criteria and policies to reward K-16 work (Tompkins, 1999).

Even more encouraging are recent efforts to acknowledge and begin reform of our graduate programs (see, e.g., Nyquist et al., 1999). A Ph.D. has never meant an entitlement to an academic job, and accordingly, it should not be so narrowly focused as to imply that academe is the only acceptable outlet for those trained in our graduate programs. Yet, as we move into the new millennium, we are only now beginning to reassess our priorities and the long-term viability of the doctoral degree.

These are positive steps forward and reflect what many of us hope will be a growing movement for how we change our academic policies and practices.

They are responses to internal pressures from our students and driven by budget and responsible management practices. But they are probably even more responses to external forces such as current economics, the general public, legislators, and those we would wish to attract as students. So, to answer the question of whose responsibility it is to train teachers, I would have to agree with Tompkins (1999) and others: There must be a strong and well-supported collaboration between faculty in the arts and sciences, in the schools of education, and in the K-12 classrooms for real progress to occur. If arts and sciences faculty are dismayed by the quality of the product that is sent to them from the high schools, they must be willing to acknowledge that they are partly to blame, and they must be willing to put their talents and creativity to work to design solutions to this problem.

WHAT ROLE SHOULD ARTS AND SCIENCES PLAY IN THIS PROCESS?

Rather than continue to lay blame, we must begin to remediate and then continue to improve the educational infrastructure across the United States at all levels. As mentioned in the preceding section, some changes are currently being tested and implemented. Strong ties need to be forged between the collaborative trio: arts and sciences, education, and K-12. In this effort, schools of education can best reach out in both directions and thus should be pivotal in establishing the connections. It is at this juncture that deans can play a significant role and a unified college of arts and sciences can be a valuable asset within a large university. The challenges for universities that have fractured the arts and sciences into separate colleges with individual deans will still be determined, at least in part, by the willingness of the respective deans to foster real collaborations.

Good working relationships between the deans of arts and sciences and education can send a strong message to faculty who are contemplating involvement in teacher preparation or enhancement activities. Joint support for providing the resources necessary to embark on interesting pilot projects or to accumulate preliminary data for funding opportunities will reinforce the message that these are valued and valuable activities.

At the University of Kansas, there is a long and successful tradition of faculty holding joint appointments, across disciplines and departments within a particular school or college, but also across the boundaries of schools and the college of arts and sciences. There are several formal joint appointments between faculty in arts and sciences departments and the school of education, and a growing number of arts and sciences departments are requesting tenure-track "educational specialist" faculty who will collaborate extensively with the education school faculty on pedagogy, curriculum design, good teaching practices, and the like, with a particular focus on their specialty discipline within the arts and sciences. At this point, gaining tenure has not been problematic for these faculty, as we have worked hard to define the criteria for tenure in each of these cases from the outset. Nor have the arts and sciences departments had to compromise significantly on promotion and tenure criteria because teaching, scholarship, and service remain the focal points for assessment. Learning to appreciate the scholarship of the educational specialist has been the challenge for arts and sciences faculty; however, as long as there is a record of active publication and, where appropriate, grant-writing activity, these cases are no more difficult to consider than any other case for promotion and tenure.

The more aware and involved that arts and sciences faculty become regarding their role in training teachers, the more likely it is that efforts to prepare better teachers (and thus students) will succeed. Indeed, motivation toward this goal need not be completely altruistic, as better prepared teachers necessarily will result in better prepared undergraduate students, something we all wish for, particularly in public institutions of higher education.

All arts and sciences faculty cannot (and should not) be actively involved in this arena, but those who are, and those who are successfully publishing, teaching, and writing grants as educational professionals, should be rewarded and praised just as we would reward and praise any faculty member who was exceeding the expectations of the job.

Despite my statements to the contrary, for some in the arts and sciences, learning to value the work of an educational specialist will not come easily. As dean, even when I knew that a department would be well served to hire such an individual, I have waited patiently for the request to come from the department. Fortunately, my patience has been rewarded, and the "peer pressure" exerted among science departments is opening the doors to more and more of these types of opportunities.

At Kansas, we also now allow tenured faculty to redefine their "work" contracts. Consequently, and for example, we have a more senior science faculty member who has discovered that he enjoys collaborating with education school faculty and writing educationally directed grants to the National Science Foundation (NSF) more than writing research-only grants to the NSF. His success rate in obtaining grants has improved dramatically by pursuing this new direction, his level of job satisfaction is once again high, and his department chair has in good conscience been encouraging his efforts with healthy merit salary increases and other types of rewards. Although purely anecdotal, this type of example illustrates the power that we can give to faculty to make significant changes in their own careers and in the lives of others.

DO COLLEGES OF LIBERAL ARTS AND SCIENCES NEED SCHOOLS OF EDUCATION?

When asked this question, the average arts and sciences faculty member is most likely to answer no. Clearly, we can be fine teachers without the proscribed regimentation of an education school curriculum. Although this cannot be interpreted in any other way than as arrogance, it is perhaps important at this point to examine why the answer is offered so quickly and usually with little or no reflection on the significance of the answer or the offense it might pose to those who are trained educational professionals.

I have often heard graduate students and even colleagues suggest that teacher shortages could be met and/or the profession improved if only we would allow our master's and Ph.D. graduates to simply "enter the profession." Given the arguments that I laid out in the preceding sections, this is indeed an arrogant and ill-informed view. It would be entirely irresponsible for schools of education to allow such a thing to happen, although why this is irresponsible would be debated differently across the academy.

For example, from the arts and sciences perspective, it is demeaning for well-trained master's and Ph.D.-level students in the various disciplines to be made to enroll in education courses designed for undergraduates on their way to becoming teachers. At the same time, I would argue that our graduate students would be well served by some degree of formal instruction and the experience that faculty in schools of education could offer. So, we need then to determine how to get these two faculties together to construct a mutually beneficial curriculum that would allow for the possibility of teacher credentialing among arts and sciences graduate students that does not embarrass the profession or demean the skills and qualities of students bright enough to be admitted to graduate programs across the academy.

At many institutions, my own included, we are at a critical juncture in terms of redefining graduate education. Never before has timing been so fortuitous as to provide the opportunity for significant dialog between those who would provide graduate education in arts and sciences and how such efforts might lead to actual credentialing of teachers who could be both qualified and prepared to teach at any level, from K through 16+.

A CALL FOR ACTION

Investing in teacher preparation is not an optional activity that we can choose to participate in or not. It is an imperative for the health and well-being of the nation and for those who will follow us into the educational arena in the future.

The primary challenge for addressing the opportunities involved in teacher preparation revolve first and foremost around good communication and collaboration between the trio of stakeholders mentioned previously—faculty and administrators from the arts and sciences, education, and K-12. As a model, I propose that examination of the graduate and undergraduate curricula take place for the express purpose of creating opportunities for graduate and undergraduate students to pursue career paths as educators at any level from K through 16+. Faculty must be involved in this endeavor, and it must be a collaboration of faculty from the trio of stakeholders, who are respected among their peers and can constructively and collaboratively suggest reforms.

In the preceding pages, I have also suggested a number of other ways in which inroads within the arts and sciences and teacher preparation can occur, and I would urge that when the opportunity for dialog and the sharing of ideas and actions is available to us, we make the effort to both listen and formulate actions. It is no accident that federal agencies, national organizations, and even accrediting agencies (Dill, 1998) are paying close attention to these issues and investing heavily in efforts that propose significant changes in the way academic educational training is conducted. In the arts and sciences, we have much to learn about educating educators, and I firmly believe that we can and will meet this challenge.

REFERENCES

Bell, J. A., & Buccino, A. (1997). *Seizing opportunities: Collaborating for excellence in teacher preparation.* Washington, DC: AAAS.
Collaboratives for Excellence in Teacher Preparation (CETP). (1998, April). *NSF collaboratives for excellence in teacher preparation: Guidelines for reform.* Paper presented at the fourth annual meeting, Arlington, VA. Published by Montana State University, Bozeman.
Dill, W. R. (1998, November/December). Guard dogs or guide dogs? Adequacy vs. quality in the accreditation of teacher education. *Change,* 13-17.
Nyquist, J. D., Manning, L., Wulff, D. H., Austin, A. E., Sprague, J., Fraser, P. K., Calcagno, C., & Woodford, B. (1999, May/June). On the road to becoming a professor: The graduate student experience. *Change,* 18-27.
Tompkins, D. (1999). Solving a "higher ed tough one." *AAHE Bulletin, 51,* 11-13.

Developing Knowledge for Preparing Teachers: Redefining the Role of Schools of Education

DENNIS THIESSEN

Within the search for a new relevance for higher education, the press to recast the long-standing commitment to knowledge development has provided schools of education with an opportunity to redefine teacher preparation. Knowledge development increasingly involves not only generating but also applying, integrating, and transforming knowledge; is pursued by more and more individuals and organizations outside universities; and has become a framework for both an expanded research agenda and program renewal. This article examines how the reconceptualization of knowledge development has influenced the structures and strategies used by schools of education to help beginning teachers build a knowledgeable start to their careers.

IN THE EARLY 1990s, Michael Fullan (1993) proclaimed that, "Teacher education still has the honor of being simultaneously the worst problem and the best solution in education" (p. 105). Later in the decade, he and his colleagues in *The Rise and Stall of Teacher Education Reform* (Fullan, Galluzo, Morris, & Watson, 1998) characterized the period between 1985 and 1995 "as a series of false starts in reform of teacher education-promises that could not be maintained" (p. xv). Less frequently stated but understood by many critics is the belief that schools of education are the primary sources of what both impedes and can propel significant changes in the preparation of teachers. The problems are of their own making, the stall is theirs to overcome, and the solutions are theirs to find.

EDUCATIONAL POLICY, Vol. 14 No. 1, January and March 2000 129-144
© 2000 Corwin Press, Inc.

Nowhere is the frustration about the lack of progress in university-based reform in teacher education more evident and nowhere have the consequences been so severe for universities than in England.[1] Wilkin (1999) summarizes the extent to which universities no longer have a prominent voice in many teacher education decisions:

Higher education institutions engaged in the professional preparation of student teachers are now subject to an unprecedented degree of central control. From before students enter the training institution, throughout their course, until they leave, few decisions are left to the members of those institutions. The numbers of students who may be recruited in each subject are passed down to the higher education institutions from the Teacher Training Agency. Selection criteria for applicants are clearly set out. Once enrolled in an institution, students will follow a course that is heavily prescribed in all its aspects: the length of the training period; the age ranges for which the student can be prepared; the time the student will spend in school; and the content of the curriculum both in general and in subject areas. The National Curriculum for teacher training has made a first appearance. The institutions are told, in exacting detail, what skills and expertise in the teaching of English and math primary students are to acquire, and the issues and ideas to which they are to be introduced. Teacher training has become painting by numbers or rather learning to teach by numbers; and moreover, institutions are to be checked to see whether they are painting carefully and accurately within the lines. . . . Three themes run through the series of government directives: first the enforced reduction in the educational contribution of the institutions to teacher education, second the attempt to control the form of that input, and third, the monitoring of compliance. (pp. 3, 8)

Whereas in England, the tendency has been to restrict and regulate the role of universities, in the United States, the approach has been to prod and press universities into action. The follow-up work of the National Commission on Teaching & America's Future (NCTAF) and the National Partnership for Excellence and Accountability in Teaching (U.S. Department of Education, 1997) illustrate two initiatives in which universities in cooperation with other key educational groups have an opportunity to transform the education of teachers through decisive acts (e.g., accreditation for all schools of education, standards for teaching, professional standards boards in every state) and bold innovations in program and policy. More recently, however, the balance has shifted to pressure university presidents especially to give greater priority to improving teacher education (U.S. Department of Education, 1998). In his annual State of American Education speech, the U.S. Secretary of Education Richard Riley stated,

We are well past the time when our institutions of higher education can remain aloof from the task of helping to rebuild America's public education system. . . . Our colleges of education can no longer be the sleepy backwaters that many of them have been. . . . There must be greater collaboration from all parts of the university community. (Basinger, 1999, p. A31)

Amid these adjustments and challenges, university-based teacher educators have scrambled to defend or redefine their once taken-for-granted primacy in the preparation of teachers (Furlong & Smith, 1996; Roth, 1999a). Despite their different circumstances and history (Grimmett & Wideen, 1995; Judge, Lemosse, Paine, & Sedlak, 1994), academics on both sides of the Atlantic resort to similar and familiar arguments to remake their case for a distinct and an essential role in teacher education. The following excerpts outline some of these positions.

United States:

[The] university purpose is to educate in a variety of modes and domains, such as critical thinking, perceiving, analyzing, reflecting, developing beliefs and values both in varied disciplines and in personal philosophy; understanding the self; and greater intellectual and psychological maturity. Collectively these areas . . . are what the university is intended for, does best, and accomplishes greater than any other institution. (Roth, 1999b, pp. 188-189)

What, then, is distinctive about the contributions of a school of education? Good schools of education provide substantive expertise for education practitioners, policy makers, and researchers. . . . Four areas of educational knowledge frame the distinctive contributions of the professional school. . . . These areas of growing knowledge and expertise, more than any others, provide the raison d'être for the education school:

• Special Knowledge About Children and Their Learning
• Special Knowledge About Knowledge Needed by the Next Generation
• Special Knowledge About Education Systems
• Special Knowledge About Culture and Young People's Learning (Holmes Group, 1995, p. 28)

If universities are to continue to make the important contribution to the education of teachers that they can make, they need to pursue these ideals of knowledge-building and truth-finding by creating a genuine praxis between ideas and experiences—by honoring practice in conjunction with reflection and research and by helping teachers reach beyond their personal boundaries to appreciate the perspectives of those whom they would teach. (Darling-Hammond, 1999, p. 28)

England:

The teacher must be a reflective practitioner whose practice is informed by theory and the university's distinctive contribution is that it ensures that teachers are educated and trained in a manner which develops their capabilities as perceptive and critical specialists who think carefully about the nature and quality of the learning experiences they provide for children. (McNamara, 1996, p. 182)

Higher Education should provide an environment in which it is possible for trainees to study core academic subjects to a high standard and to develop knowledge and understanding about different methods of teaching and the ways in which children learn. It should provide the context in which trainees develop an ability to think critically about, and reflect on, teaching practice and provide breadth of perspective, as well as exposure to other disciplines and access to pedagogic research. Higher education should also have a role in training teaching mentors and providing continuing professional development that builds upon initial teacher training. (Sutherland, 1997, p. 17)

In sum, the university represents a tradition of critical enquiry and research. Such a tradition is essential to the education of the next generation of teachers, but it must *serve the profession* in its exercise of responsibility for initial training—a more subservient but essential role, different from that in which universities have traditionally controlled the training with little reference to the teachers and the schools themselves. The partnership has to be a real one with the distinctive expertise and contributions spelt out. (Pring, in press)

At first blush, these quotations are an attempt to reclaim a higher ground in which scholars pursue knowledge through a persistent and critical discourse and inquiry that universities have long revered. Such an environment enables beginning teachers[2] to develop the kind of intellectual edge they need to understand and enact their professional responsibilities. Some of the above statements (notably by Darling-Hammond, 1999, and Pring, in press) reveal a pursuit of knowledge developed within and for the improvement of practice, an emerging agenda shared by universities and schools alike. In this world, beginning teachers learn by participating in this grounded and collaborative knowledge development process. It is in the search for the common ground and in the more inclusive and responsive engagement with knowledge that schools of education can rediscover their niche in the preparation of teachers.

In the rest of the article, I begin by situating this new knowledge development agenda within the changing directions of higher education. I then examine the implications of this new agenda for schools of education, with a particular emphasis on the relocated and reconceptualized part they can have in the design and delivery of teacher education programs. The concluding section takes up the transformative possibilities for schools of education committed to developing knowledge for preparing teachers, an opportunity not to be missed; otherwise, they will be missed in the opportunity.

KNOWLEDGE DEVELOPMENT
AND UNIVERSITIES

The search for what universities bring to the teacher education table is occurring amid a wider deliberation about a new compact between higher education and the many communities it serves (National Committee of Inquiry into Higher Learning, 1997). Within the many calls for a new relevance (Gibbons, 1998) for and a reconstructed engagement (National Association of State Universities and Land-Grant Colleges [NASULGC], 1999) by higher education, two shifts in the long-standing commitment of universities to the development of knowledge are important to note. First, although universities have historically devoted considerable effort to the generation of knowledge, there is a growing demand and comparable status for integrating, applying, and transforming (through teaching) knowledge (Boyer, 1990). Second, although their prominent place in knowledge production is still evident, more and more individuals and organizations outside the universities are involved in every aspect of how knowledge is created, used, and extended.

In considering the various knowledge missions of universities, Walshok (1995, p. 156) emphasizes applying and testing knowledge, transmitting and diffusing knowledge, and dialoguing and interacting with knowledge stakeholders more than discovering new knowledge, developing knowledge, and collecting, organizing, and preserving knowledge. Gibbons (1998) goes further by giving priority to knowledge reconfiguration and calling on universities "to take the lead in the training of knowledge workers—individuals who are skilled and creative at making use of knowledge that may have been produced anywhere in a global distributed knowledge system" (p. 60). Generating knowledge is still important but more embedded in and emergent from the more pressing need to make use of what is already known. Consequently, as knowledge workers (e.g., beginning teachers) reconfigure (integrate, apply, transform) knowledge, further ideas emerge; concepts are revisited, critiqued, and elaborated; and, eventually, new knowledge is discovered and reconfigured again.

The increased attention to integrating, applying, and transforming knowledge also comes with changes in what the knowledge is for and how and with whom it develops. Universities must seek knowledge that helps others respond to the most urgent and compelling problems of the day (e.g., in the case of schools of education, knowledge that would assist teachers in improving their practice). Such knowledge is more likely developed *out there*, initially and continually negotiated with those for whom it most matters. It is dynamic, evolves in the context of use, and is shaped by the expertise from various disciplines on campus and by those in the field who take up, adapt, and probe the knowledge and its value to their work.

In this more responsive agenda, knowledge development thus requires a different relationship between universities and its many communities, one founded on mutual regard and reciprocity. The Kellogg Commission on the Future of State and Land-Granted Universities sees this partnership as one of the guiding characteristics of an *engaged institution*:

> The purpose of engagement is not to provide the university's superior expertise to the community but to encourage joint academic-community definitions of problems, solutions, and definitions of success. Here we need to ask ourselves if our institutions genuinely respect the skills and capacities of our partners in collaborative projects. In a sense we are asking that we recognize fully that we have almost as much to learn in these efforts as we have to offer. (NASULGC, 1999, p. 12)

Engagement goes well beyond conventional strategies of one-way and short-term service and outreach by individual professors. Instead, universities establish a web of team-like relationships across departments (transdisciplinarity—see Gibbons, 1998, p. 7) and contexts (e.g., linking schools of education to elementary and high schools) to tackle the persistent and fundamental problems in society, a challenge that depends on the collaborative capacity of this network of (university-based and school-based) knowledge workers for success.

With all forms of scholarship—generating, integrating, applying, and transforming knowledge—universities, then, are deeply connected with their constituents. For the preparation of teachers, this in particular means partnerships in which schools of education (representing and coordinating the contributions of higher education) join with their professional colleagues in schools. In this knowledge-based connectedness, the role of schools of education is less about providing the skills and theories that beginning teachers apply and practice in the field (Wideen, Mayer-Smith, & Moon, 1998) or even sorting out how the respective expertise offered on campus and in schools can coexist (Fenstermacher, 1994; McNamara, 1996). These stances can perpetuate the privileged or separate perch of universities[3] and diminish the dialectical possibilities of more intensive and inclusive higher education–school partnerships. Instead of remaining outside and apart from those in schools, university-based teacher educators see themselves as part of the same professional community. Creating partnerships amounts to reaching out to those within, but in a different neighborhood of, an educational community they share and support. In preparing teachers, these partners work as peers, university-based and school-based teacher educators, whose particular understandings of teaching and learning to teach interact and build the program beginning teachers' experience.[4]

KNOWLEDGE DEVELOPMENT
IN TEACHER EDUCATION

The National Commission on Teaching & America's Future (1996) frames a number of its proposals for reinventing teacher preparation in terms of access to and the acquisition of knowledge (e.g., "more knowledge about curriculum and assessment design"). It describes the types of knowledge required and a promising structure (professional development schools) within which to develop this knowledge:

Successful teacher preparation programs aim to develop a foundation for continual learning about teaching—the capacity to analyze learning and examine the effects of contexts and teaching strategies on students' motivation, interest, and achievement—rather than aiming only to transmit techniques for managing daily classroom activities. This requires building a strong foundation of knowledge about learning, development, motivation, and behavior, including their cognitive, social and cultural bases. It also requires creating cases and other inquiries that allow students to use this knowledge in applied contexts—to gather information, analyze and learn from their knowledge, and use what they have learned to assess situations and improve instruction. This kind of preparation is essential if teachers are to work productively with diverse learners. (p. 77)

[Professional development schools are like] teaching hospitals in medicine. [They] provide new recruits with sites for intensively supervised internships where they can experience state-of-the-art-practice that is linked to their coursework. They also provide sites for research by school- and university-based faculty, creating more powerful knowledge for teaching by putting research into practice and practice into research. (p. 80)

Learning to teach is about the development of professional knowledge (Borko & Putnam, 1996; Calderhead, 1996; Carter, 1990; Eraut, 1994; Feiman-Nemser & Remillard, 1996; Mumby, Russell, & Martin, in press). Professional knowledge involves the interrelationship of practical (e.g., routines, procedures, methods) and propositional (e.g., discipline-based frameworks and concepts, pedagogical principles, situation-specific theories) knowledge. Beginning teachers have to develop their capacity to concurrently use both kinds of knowledge in an integrated and purposeful manner. Various concepts or frameworks (propositional knowledge) can be used to guide planning, to provide an alternative exploration for why certain classroom experiences occurred, or to evaluate the success of a particular approach (practical knowledge). Similarly, many trial-and-error cycles, confrontations with different incidents of the same problem, or continuous adjustments of preferred strategies in specific situations (practical knowledge) can generate, modify, or reshape the structure and content of related theories (propositional knowledge). The core program challenge is to devise opportunities for beginning teachers that compel and stimulate their ability to concurrently use practical and propositional knowledge.

The key components of a teacher education program designed to respond to this knowledge development challenge are suggested by the changing directions in higher education (see previous section) and the emerging concept of professional knowledge. In preparing teachers for a knowledgeable start to their career, program strategies need to concentrate on experiences that

1. involve all four forms of knowledge development: generating, integrating, applying, and transforming knowledge;
2. invoke the combined use of both practical and propositional knowledge; and
3. focus on the persistent and fundamental problems, incidents, or phenomena in classroom and school practice.

Furthermore, these three components require the participation of both university-based and school-based teacher educators in campus and school activities to link and integrate the knowledge beginning teachers develop in each setting. Although the emphasis varies—stressing practically relevant propositional knowledge on campus and propositionally relevant practical knowledge in schools—the consistent and cohering image is one of teaching and learning to teach as knowledge development.[5]

At the university, beginning teachers develop practically relevant propositional knowledge through approaches that engage beginning teachers in different forms of knowledge development. Table 1 identifies three pedagogical frames and the corresponding knowledge development process.

Numerous laboratory and clinical activities help beginning teachers explore the practical relevance of propositional knowledge (McIntyre, Byrd, & Fox, 1996; Winitzky & Arends, 1991). Howey (1996) lists a number of

Table 1
Pedagogical Frames and Corresponding Knowledge Development in Universities

Pedagogical Frame	Primary Form of Knowledge Development
Studying about practice	Integrating knowledge
Observing and trying out practice under simulated conditions	Applying and transforming knowledge
Comparing and elaborating practice for classrooms	Integrating and generating knowledge

activities to foster critical teaching abilities in pedagogical laboratories (which I have reorganized according to the above pedagogical frames):

Studying About Practice

- case development and analyses
- interactive problem analyses using computers
- remote viewing of teaching and learning with subsequent analysis

Observing and Trying Out Practice
Under Simulated Conditions

- clinical diagnoses and child study employing one-way mirrors
- structural observation and analyses of videotaped teaching and learning
- simulation of a number of types (e.g., typical incidents)
- micro-reflective teaching in peer groups
- teaching clinic—either expert teacher analyzes teaching for novice or novice teacher analyzes teaching for expert

Comparing and Elaborating Practice for Classrooms
- professional profile and portfolio development

In these strategies, beginning teachers work through how best to relate propositions about teaching to the practical skills and reasoning they will need for their complex, dynamic, and often unpredictable life in classrooms.

Propositional knowledge in these campus experiences has at least four functions: to (a) guide what beginning teachers learn, (b) offer a lens through which to analyze reproduced or reconstructed accounts of practice, (c) act as benchmarks for assessing the application of certain approaches in controlled (time, pace, place, form) situations, and (d) provide departure points for the development of more personalized theories about teaching. In terms of concurrent use, propositional and practical knowledge intersect, initially in a

Table 2
Pedagogical Frames and Corresponding Knowledge Development in Schools

Pedagogical Frame	Primary Form of Knowledge Development
Observing and trying out practice under actual conditions	Applying and transforming knowledge
Comparing and elaborating practice in classrooms	Transforming and generating knowledge
Deliberating about practice	Integrating and generating knowledge

manner in which practical knowledge is derived from propositional knowledge, but over time, amid the kind of intellectual discourse suggested above by Howey (1996) (and through comparisons with field-based knowledge development, see below), beginning teachers draw on their growing practical knowledge to reference and, where justified, adapt their propositional knowledge. This knowledge interchange takes a different turn when it moves from the contrived and contemplative problems of the laboratory to the spontaneous and polysynchronous problems of the classroom.

In schools, beginning teachers develop propositionally relevant practical knowledge through approaches that are similar in purpose to the three pedagogical frames used on campus but different in the extent to which certain forms of knowledge development are pursued. Beginning teachers have more chances to transform what they know in practice (first two frames) and, in reflecting in and on these actions (Schon, 1983), to generate further insight into teaching and learning in the classroom (second and third frames, see Table 2).

In the changing circumstances of classroom life, beginning teachers experience routine and disruption, familiar and unique situations, and predictable and unpredictable incidents. These swings often expose the taken-for-granted assumptions beginning teachers bring to the job. As they learn to cope with this naturally unfolding world, they make their implicit ideas explicit and, where necessary, alter them to correspond to their revised practices. Whether motivated by a field-based assignment or a desire for self-improvement, beginning teachers also confront persistent problems in the classroom by testing out alternative approaches or probing further into conditions that directly or indirectly affect their actions. Through sustained time in classrooms, beginning teachers have many opportunities to generate and refine their own practical knowledge in a way that remains mindful of the relationship to their evolving propositional knowledge.

When learning from within the action, propositional knowledge is more in the background, often in the crevices of beginning teachers' implicit theories.

When involved in observing and trying out practice under more managed classroom conditions (e.g., working with small groups or for a segment of a lesson only), however, propositional knowledge can interact with practical knowledge in ways that are similar to its functions on campus (as a guide to learning, a lens for analysis, a benchmark in assessment, or a point from which to personalize practice). Schools also create deliberative moments (the school-based version of studying about practice on campus) in which in weekly seminars, workshops, or problem-solving clinics (Cohn, Gellman, & Tom, 1987; Lemlech & Hertzog-Foliart, 1993; Stallings, 1991; Thomson, Beacham, & Misulis, 1992), beginning teachers pause to discuss the dynamic complexity of classrooms with university-based and school-based teacher educators. Here, propositional knowledge coexists with practical knowledge with beginning teachers alternatively using one as a foil for the other, each as a particular vantage point from which to view and make sense of the events of the day or both to mutually inform their subsequent teaching decisions.

The traditional dominance of propositional knowledge on campus, and on practical knowledge in schools, persists. The above strategic directions (practically relevant propositional knowledge and propositionally relevant practical knowledge), however, ensure that beginning teachers have numerous opportunities to concurrently use these two types of knowledge in each setting. Yet, for professional knowledge first encountered and developed in one context to be used in another context, further adaptation and even relearning need to occur. The coordinated initiatives of university-based and school-based teacher educators in both contexts are the critical force in supporting these transitions and translations between the learning of beginning teachers on campus and in schools. They can develop activities that ask beginning teachers to link their learning to teach across both contexts (e.g., maintaining of portfolio of their professional learning in all facets of the program). They can design more robust and enabling environments for connecting practical and propositional knowledge (e.g., pedagogical laboratories in universities [see Howey, 1996; McIntyre et al., 1996]; and professional development schools in the field [see Levine & Trachtman, 1997; Valli, Cooper, & Frances, 1997]). They can organize programs by unifying images of teaching and learning to teach (e.g., constructivism—see Richardson, 1997).[6] Through such pedagogical, structural, and conceptual strategies, teacher education programs add further platforms for stimulating and interrelating knowledge development.

On campus and in schools, the knowledge development of beginning teachers requires all three pedagogical frames: some time away from the action to study about anticipated practice and to reflect back on transpired practice, some opportunities to try out and adjust practice under relatively risk-free situations, and some situations to extend and to refine their skill and understanding through repeated and prolonged considerations about (at universities) and engagement in the compelling problems of practice (in classrooms). At every pedagogical turn, beginning teachers generate, integrate, apply, or transform some blend of their evolving practical and prepositional knowledge. Their professional (knowledge) development is what preparing teachers is about.

A NECESSARY BUT DIFFERENT ROLE
FOR SCHOOLS OF EDUCATION

The above knowledge development agenda for schools of education represents a shift from a distinct but less necessary role to a necessary but less distinct role in the preparation of teachers. Interestingly, some of the traditionally hallowed grounds of higher education remain largely unchallenged. Most support the need for teachers, like members of other professions, to complete undergraduate degrees. Despite an increasingly diverse cast in continuing professional education, many look to universities to provide avenues for further graduate study. In a "distributed knowledge production system" (Gibbons, 1998, p. i), there still is a high regard for the primary if not lead role of universities in generating new knowledge. Schools of education share in each of these relatively uncontested sources of status and expertise. Where they do come under more criticism is in the debate over the nature and value of how schools of education approach teacher education and the extent to which they should influence the major decisions in teacher preparation. Attempts by schools of education to privilege propositional knowledge, to defend their production rights to knowledge teachers need to acquire, or to control program decisions have prompted some critics to conclude that such distinct contributions are less necessary. Schools of education become necessary when they are less preoccupied with their exclusive and unique place in teacher education and more focused on extending their "role from that of creator and transmitter of generalizable knowledge to that of *enhancing the knowledge creation capacities* of individuals and professional communities" (Eraut, 1994, p. 57).

Clearly, a distinct role for schools of education is part of the new knowledge development agenda but one that recasts enduring strengths within a more connected relationship with the wider education community. As Pring (in press) summarizes,

These then seem to be the distinctive and necessary contributions of higher education—a distinctive kind of knowledge within the practical deliberation of practical know-how, a nurturing of that "pedagogical subject knowledge," the provision and maintenance of a critical tradition, and the provision of (and making accessible) relevant research. What is not the case is (but what is commonly believed) that universities are good at what teachers are good at—at the practice teaching. Rather have they a more subservient, though crucial, role, one which is put at the service of teachers and then only in partnership with them. And it brings with it certain responsibilities—in particular, the responsibility to create the conditions in which teachers share in and contribute their own distinctive expertise to the development of knowledge.

University-based teacher educators then work with school-based teacher educators in a collaborative and co-constructed pursuit of answers to significant questions about beginning teacher learning. In this process, they concurrently use and combine their respective practical and propositional knowledge (e.g., about how teachers learn, which pedagogical strategies are appropriate for what purposes, which structural arrangement best supports certain forms of development) to generate, integrate, apply, and transform what matters in teacher education programs. Those in schools of education find themselves in a different sociopolitical location in which knowledge development is more interdependent than independent, more integrated than differentiated, more negotiated than directed, and more embedded than detached. Their relocation carries an obligation to lead the wider professional community in an ongoing knowledge-based improvement in the preparation of teachers. In so doing, schools of education trade distinctiveness for the distinction that comes from creating more relevant and impactful programs for beginning teachers.

NOTES

1. I refer to a number of sources that comment on the role of universities in England and the United States to elaborate particular issues and directions, not to compare the two countries. Nonetheless, the respective points of view emanating from these two regions do remind us about the global challenges we often share.

2. I prefer the term *beginning teachers* to identify students in initial teacher preparation programs.

3. In a more distributed and interrelated system of knowledge development, universities may still take the lead in but are no longer the exclusive preserve of theoretical discourse and critical inquiry. These norms permeate and evolve within the partnerships that schools of education establish with the wider educational community.

4. Furlong et al. (1996) differentiate three models of partnership: (a) higher education institution–led, (b) separatist, and (c) collaborative. The collaborative partnership, exemplified by the secondary postgraduate certificate in education program in Oxford (McIntyre & Hagger, 1992), has some features similar to the knowledge-based connections proposed in this article, namely, an integrated curriculum, complementarity in roles, and access to different kinds of knowledge.

5. A pedagogical portrayal of practically relevant propositional knowledge and propositionally relevant practical knowledge is available in an article in the *International Journal of Education Research* (Thiessen, in press). There, I argue that developing professional knowledge is the most recent orientation to supporting a skillful start to a teaching career, incorporating and transforming two more long-standing traditions—the skill acquisition and use orientation, and the thoughtful development of teaching processes orientation.

6. See Arends and Winitzky (1996) for a critical review of the value of program themes.

REFERENCES

Arends, R., & Winitzky, N. (1996). Program structures and learning to teach. In F. Murray (Ed.), *The teacher educator's handbook* (pp. 526-556). San Francisco: Jossey-Bass.

Basinger, J. (1999, February 26). Riley calls on college leaders to improve teacher education. *The Chronicle of Higher Education, 45*(25), A31.

Borko, H., & Putnam, R. (1996). Learning to teach. In D. C. Berliner & R. C. Calfee (Eds.), *Handbook of educational psychology* (pp. 673-708). New York: Macmillan.

Boyer, E. (1990). *Scholarship reconsidered: Priorities of the professoriate.* Princeton, NJ: Carnegie Foundation for the Advancement of Teaching.

Calderhead, J. (1996). Teachers: Beliefs and knowledge. In D. C. Berliner & R. C. Calfee (Eds.), *Handbook of educational psychology* (pp. 709-725). New York: Macmillan.

Carter, K. (1990). Teachers' knowledge and learning to teach. In W. R. Houston (Ed.), *Handbook of research on teacher education* (pp. 291-310). New York: Macmillan.

Cohn, M., Gellman, V., & Tom, A. (1987). The secondary professional semester. *Teaching Education, 1*(2), 31-37.

Darling-Hammond, L. (1999). The case for university-based teacher education. In R. Roth (Ed.), *The role of the university in the preparation of teachers* (pp. 13-30). London: Falmer.

Eraut, M. (1994). *Developing professional knowledge and competence.* London: Falmer.

Feiman-Nemser, S., & Remillard, J. (1996). Perspectives on learning to teach. In F. Murray (Ed.), *The teacher educator's handbook* (pp. 63-91). San Francisco: Jossey-Bass.

Fenstermacher, G. (1994). *Where are we going? Who will lead us there?* Presidential address to the meeting of the American Association for Colleges of Teacher Education, San Antonio, Texas.

Fullan, M. (1993). *Change forces: Probing the depths of educational reform.* London: Falmer.

Fullan, M., Galluzzo, G., Morris, P., & Watson, N. (1998). *The rise and stall of teacher education reform.* Washington, DC: American Association of Colleges for Teacher Education.

Furlong, J., & Smith, R. (Eds.). (1996). *The role of higher education in initial teacher training.* London: Kogan Page.

Furlong, J., Whitty, G., Witing, C., Miles, S., Barton, L., & Barrett, E. (1996). Re-defining partnership: Revolution or reform in teacher education? *Journal of Education for Teaching, 22*(1), 35-55.

Gibbons, M. (1998, October 8). *Higher education relevance in the 21st century.* Paper presented to the UNESCO World Conference on Higher Education, Paris, France.

Grimmett, P., & Wideen, M. (Eds.). (1995). *Changing times in teacher education: Restructuring or reconceptualization?* London: Falmer.

Holmes Group. (1995). *Tomorrow's schools of education.* East Lansing, MI: Author.

Howey, K. (1996). Designing coherent and effective teacher education programs. In J. Sikula, T. Buttery, & E. Guyton (Eds.), *Handbook of research on teacher education* (2nd ed., pp. 143-170). New York: Macmillan.

Judge, H., Lemosse, M., Paine, L., & Sedlak, M. (1994). *The university and the teachers: France, the United States, England.* Wallingford, UK: Triangle.

Lemlech, J., & Hertzog-Foliart, H. (1993). Linking school and university through collegial student teaching. *Teacher Education Quarterly, 20*(4), 19-27.

Levine, M., & Trachtman, R. (Eds.). (1997). *Making professional development schools work: Politics, practice and policy.* New York: Teachers College Press.

McIntyre, D., Byrd, D., & Fox, S. (1996). Field and laboratory experiences. In J. Sikula, T. Buttery, & E. Guyton (Eds.), *Handbook of research on teacher education* (2nd ed., pp. 171-193). New York: Macmillan.

McIntyre, D., & Hagger, H. (1992). Professional development through the Oxford internship model. *British Journal of Educational Studies, 40*(3), 264-283.

McNamara, D. (1996). The university, the academic tradition and education. In J. Furlong & R. Smith (Eds.), *The role of higher education in initial teacher training* (pp. 179-194). London: Kogan Page.

Mumby, H., Russell, T., & Martin, A. (in press). Teachers' knowledge and how it develops. In V. Richardson (Ed.), *Handbook of research on teaching* (4th ed.). New York: Macmillan.

National Association of State Universities and Land-Grant Colleges. (1999). *Returning to our roots: The engaged institution.* Washington, DC: Author.

National Commission on Teaching & America's Future. (1996). *What matters most: Teaching for America's future.* Woodbridge, VA: Author.

National Committee of Inquiry into Higher Learning. (1997). *Higher education in the learning society.* London: HMSO Crown.

Pring, R. (in press). Universities and teacher education. *Higher Education Quarterly.*

Richardson, V. (Ed.). (1997). *Constructivist teacher education: Building a world of new understandings.* London: Falmer.

Roth, R. (Ed.). (1999a). *The role of the university in the preparation of teachers.* London: Falmer.

Roth, R. (1999b). University as context for teacher development. In R. Roth (Ed.), *The role of the university in the preparation of teachers* (pp. 180-195). London: Falmer.

Schon, D. A. (1983). *The reflective practitioner: How professionals think in action.* New York: Basic Books.

Stallings, J. A. (1991, April 3-7). *Connecting preservice teacher education and inservice professional development: A professional development school.* Paper presented at the annual meeting of the American Education Research Association, Chicago. (ERIC Document Reproduction Service No. 339682)

Sutherland, S. (1997). Teacher education and training: A study. In the National Committee of Inquiry Into Higher Learning (Ed.), *Higher education in the learning society.* London: HMSO Crown.

Thiessen, D. (in press). A skillful start to a teaching career: A matter of developing impactful behaviours, thoughtful practices, or professional knowledge? *International Journal of Educational Research.*

Thomson, W. S., Beacham, B. G., & Misulis, K. E. (1992). A university and public school collaborative approach to preparing elementary teachers. *The Teacher Educator, 28*(2), 46-51.

U.S. Department of Education. (1997). *A partnership of excellence and accountability: Request for proposal.* Washington, DC: Author.

U.S. Department of Education. (1998). *Promising practices: New ways to improve teacher quality.* Washington, DC: Author.

Valli, L., Cooper, D., & Frances, L. (1997). Professional development schools and equity: A critical analysis of rhetoric and research. In M. Apple (Ed.), *Review of research in education,* 22 (pp. 251-304). Washington, DC: American Educational Research Association.

Walshok, M. (1995). *Knowledge without boundaries. What America's research universities can do for the economy, the workplace, and the community.* San Francisco: Jossey-Bass.

Wideen, M., Mayer-Smith, J., & Moon, B. (1998). A critical analysis of research on learning to teach: Making the case for an ecological perspective on inquiry. *Review of Educational Research, 68*(2), 130-178.

Wilkin, M. (1999). *The role of higher education in initial teacher education* (Occasional Paper No. 12). London: Universities Council for the Education of Teachers.

Winitzky, N., & Arends, R. (1991). Translating research into practice: The effects of various forms of training and clinical experiences on preservice students' knowledge, skills, and reflectiveness. *Journal of Teacher Education, 42*(1), 52-65.

Adequacy and Allocation Within Higher Education: Funding the Work of Education Schools

RICHARD D. HOWARD, RANDY HITZ,
and LARRY J. BAKER

The perception held by many teacher educators is that the commitment by colleges and universities to education programs is weak and funding for education lags far behind that of other disciplines. This perception was validated by a national study in which expenditure data for education programs were compared to those of other academic disciplines. The results of the study are presented in this article, followed by a discussion of the role a strong national accrediting body could play in support of stronger funding for teacher education programs.

THE PERCEPTION held by many teacher educators is that the commitment of colleges and universities to education programs is weak and funding for education lags far behind that of other disciplines. In a rare study on this topic, Ebmeier, Twombly, and Teeter (1991) examined the comparability and adequacy of financial support for schools of education at six research institutions. They found that "schools of education do not hold a favorable position in the research university" (p. 226). Not only did education lag in funding behind nearly all other professional or academic programs at the universities studied, education schools had actually lost ground in comparative funding during the 10 years of the study.

Like Bowen (1980), Hample (1980), and Walters (1981), Ebmeier et al. (1991) noted that expenditure comparisons from one institution to another have rarely been undertaken because of the uniqueness of each institution's

EDUCATIONAL POLICY, Vol. 14 No. 1, January and March 2000 145-160
© 2000 Corwin Press, Inc.

financial record-keeping systems. Ebmeier et al. were able to conduct their study using peer institution data available after considerable institutional effort to define common terms. This has made large-scale expenditure comparisons extremely difficult. Our review of the literature indicated that, to date, no study has been conducted to substantiate or refute the claim that nationally, education is poorly funded relative to other professional and academic programs on college and university campuses.

In this article, the question of funding for education programs as compared to other professional disciplines is addressed. Expenditure data collected by the Office of Institutional Research and Planning (1996) at the University of Delaware (funded by a grant from the Fund to Improve Post Secondary Education [FIPSE]) were used to make the comparisons. Using standard definitions, this data collection effort resulted in the development of standardized expenditure and productivity data, at the program level, from institutions reflecting all types and sizes of colleges and universities nationally.

Initially, we present the results of research we published in fall 1998 (Howard, Hitz, & Baker, 1998), in which expenditures by discipline and institutional type are compared. To complement the findings reported in this article, comparative data about education faculty and administrative salaries and faculty productivity are presented. The article ends with a discussion about existing and potential funding sources for education programs and the realities of institutional internal reallocation to enhance support of education programs. Our intent in the article is to present the financial status of education programs in colleges and universities in comparison to programs in other disciplines and offer suggestions for why funding of education programs is relatively low.

The reader is referred to Howard et al. (1998) for an explanation of the data and methodology used to create the comparative information in which expenditures across disciplines and teacher education programs by the four Carnegie classifications for colleges and universities were developed. In addition, for a listing of the participating colleges and universities and a detailed description of the Classification of Instructional Programs (CIP) codes, see *Comparative Study of Expenditures per Student Credit Hour of Education Programs to Programs of Other Disciplines and Professions*, a report prepared for the Government Relations Committee of the American Association of Colleges for Teacher Education (AACTE), the Association of Colleges and Schools of Education in State Universities and Land Grant Colleges and Affiliated Private Universities, and the Teacher Education Council for State Colleges and Universities (Howard, Hitz, & Baker, 1997). Below (through

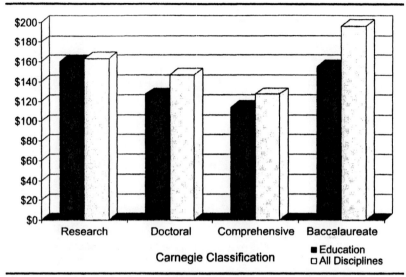

Figure 11), the results of the study are presented as they appeared in the article.

COMPARISON OF AVERAGE EXPENDITURES FOR ALL DISCIPLINES BY CARNEGIE CLASSIFICATION

Average expenditures per student credit hour (SCH) over all disciplines were compared. Consistent with earlier research (AACTE, 1987), the undergraduate average expenditures per SCH at baccalaureate institutions were the highest ($196) followed by the average expenditures at Research I and II institutions ($163), Doctoral I and II institutions ($147), and comprehensive institutions ($127). At the graduate level, overall expenditures per SCH were highest at Research I and II institutions ($272) followed by Doctoral I and II institutions ($246) and comprehensive institutions ($211) (see Figures 1 and 2).

COMPARISON OF EDUCATION EXPENDITURES TO OTHER DISCIPLINES

For each of the Carnegie classifications, education average expenditures were below the average expenditures of all disciplines. At Research I and II institutions, the average expenditure per undergraduate and graduate SCH

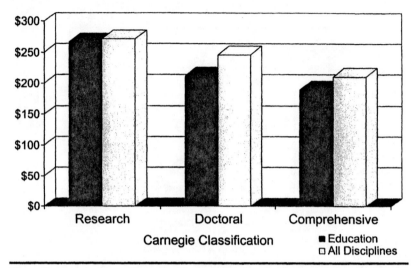

Figure 2.   Average Expenditure per Graduate Student Credit Hour for All Disciplines

for education programs was only slightly less than (98.4%) the overall average expenditure per SCH, whereas within the other Carnegie classifications, the average expenditures per undergraduate and graduate SCH for education programs ranged between 10% and 21% below the total average (see Figures 1 and 2).

VARIANCE OF EXPENDITURE PER SCH WITHIN CARNEGIE CLASSIFICATIONS

In Figures 3 and 4, the wide variance (range) of expenditures per SCH within institutional type is illustrated. It is obvious from these figures that expenditures vary greatly across all types of institutions and within institutional types. Because of these wide variances, comparisons of a particular program's average expenditure with the means presented here should be approached with caution.

COMPARISON OF AVERAGE EXPENDITURES OF EDUCATION PROGRAMS BY CARNEGIE CLASSIFICATION

The average expenditures for undergraduate and graduate SCH in education programs are illustrated by Carnegie classification in Figure 5. The

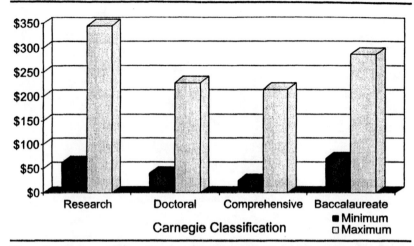

Figure 3. Variance of Expenditure per Undergraduate Student Credit Hour for Education Programs

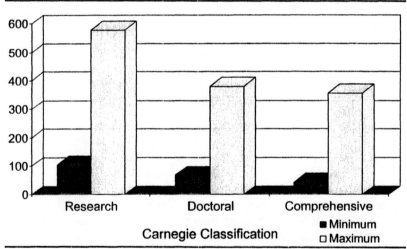

Figure 4. Variance of Expenditure per Graduate Student Credit Hour for Education Programs

average expenditure per undergraduate student credit hour (USCH) at baccalaureate institutions ranked second highest ($155), only slightly less than that at Research I and II institutions ($160). At Doctoral I and II institutions, the average expenditure per USCH was $127 and at comprehensive institutions

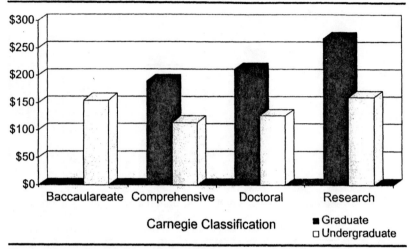

Figure 5. Average Expenditure per Student Credit Hour for Education Programs

$114. At the graduate level, the average expenditure per SCH at Research I and II institutions was $267; at Doctoral I and II institutions, $212; and at comprehensive institutions, $190.

COMPARISON OF TEACHER EDUCATION EXPENDITURES TO OTHER PROFESSIONAL DISCIPLINES

Teacher education programs were defined in this analysis as all undergraduate programs with a CIP code of 13. In Figures 6, 7, and 8, undergraduate and graduate average expenditures in education are compared to the undergraduate and graduate expenditures of other professional disciplines by Carnegie classification. It is clear from these figures that teacher education (undergraduate) expenditures per SCH are significantly less than the average expenditures per SCH of other professional programs compared in this study, ranging from 80% at Research I and II institutions to 69% at comprehensive institutions. Data were not available for professional programs other than education at the baccalaureate institutions. The relative expenditure of the various professional programs at the graduate level would be the same as that of the undergraduate level, the difference being only in the magnitude of the average expenditures. As such, the graduate-level expenditures were not graphed.

At research institutions, the total average expenditure per SCH in education is 80.6% of the mean expenditure for the seven professional programs

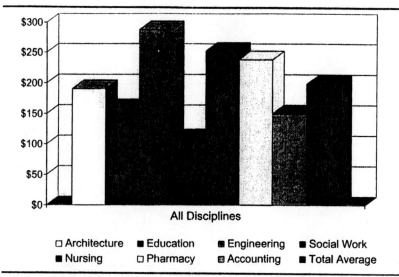

Figure 6. Average Expenditure per Undergraduate Student Credit Hour for Professional Programs at Research Institutions

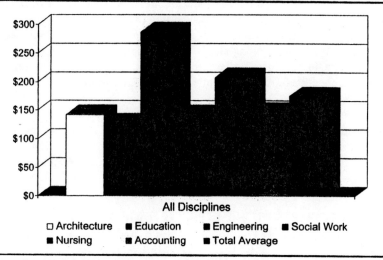

Figure 7. Average Expenditure per Undergraduate Student Credit Hour for Professional Programs at Doctoral Institutions

compared. Average expenditures per SCH in education rank fifth lowest ($160) among the seven professional programs, after engineering ($288),

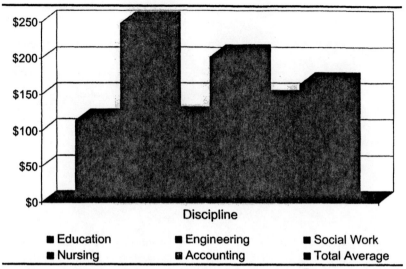

Figure 8.   **Average Expenditure per Undergraduate Student Credit Hour for Professional Programs at Comprehensive Institutions**

nursing ($252), pharmacy ($238), and architecture ($190); the two ranking lower are social work ($111) and accounting ($150) (see Figure 6).

At doctoral institutions, the total average expenditure per SCH in education ($127) is lowest among all six professional programs compared. The expenditure for engineering is $287 per SCH, nursing $127, accounting $147, architecture $142, and social work $141. Education is 74% of the total average (see Figure 7).

At comprehensive institutions, the total average expenditure per SCH in education ($114) is lowest among all five professional programs compared. Again, engineering is highest at $248 per SCH, followed by nursing at $203, accounting at $140, and social work at $117. Education is 69% of the total average for the five professional programs (see Figure 8).

COMPARISON OF THE PERCENTAGE OF GRADUATE
SCH IN PROFESSIONAL PROGRAMS BY
CARNEGIE CLASSIFICATION

Graduate programs are typically more expensive to deliver than undergraduate programs. It would stand to reason that the overall expenditure per SCH would be greater in departments with higher proportions of graduate school credit hours (GSCH) compared to USCH. This is not the case for education. With the single exception of social work at research universities, education

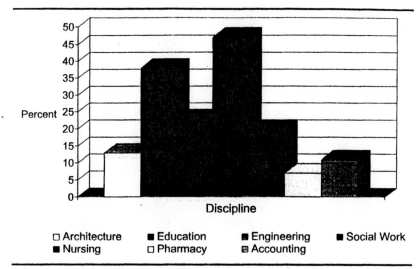

Figure 9. **Percentage of Graduate Student Credit Hour for Professional Programs at Research Institutions**

departments on average have a much higher ratio of graduate to undergraduate SCH than the other professional programs; still, the overall expenditures per SCH lag behind the other disciplines (see Figures 9, 10, and 11).

The results of the analyses presented above provide clear evidence that, in general, education programs are funded below the institutional average for all disciplines in all classifications of institutions. These findings become even more significant when characteristics of education programs, which should make them more expensive rather than less expensive, are considered. First, education programs typically include, as a percentage of total courses offered, fewer lower division (and less expensive) courses than most other higher education programs. Second, education programs are clinical in nature, including student teaching and other practicum experiences, requiring low faculty-to-student ratios, which should be more costly than typical classroom instruction. Third, education programs include a much higher percentage of graduate courses than other disciplines. Graduate programs are generally more expensive to operate because class enrollments are smaller, and graduate instruction requires faculty to be involved in the time-consuming work of advising graduate students and directing theses and dissertations.

In addition, these results also provide clear evidence that, in general, education programs are less well funded than other professional programs. Again, these findings take on additional significance as, with the single

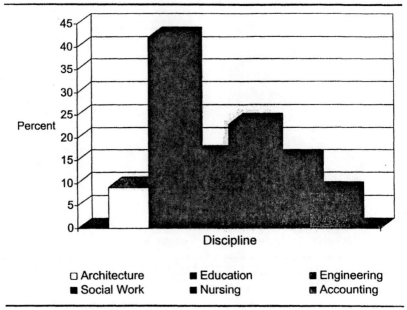

Figure 10.   Percentage of Graduate Student Credit Hours for Professional Programs at Doctoral Institutions

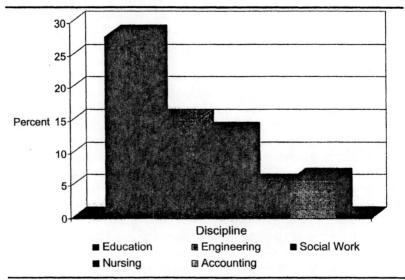

Figure 11.   Percentage of Graduate Student Credit Hours for Professional Programs at Comprehensive Institutions

Table 1

Comparison of Mean Faculty Salaries 1996-1997—Teacher Education Versus All Other Disciplines, Public and Private

	Professor	Associate Professor	Assistant Professor	New Assistant Professor	Instructor	All
Teacher education mean faculty salaries ($)						
Public	56,383	45,451	37,915	35,086	30,770	44,819
Private	54,966	43,475	36,192	34,760	30,880	42,315
All discipline mean faculty salaries ($)						
Public	64,760	49,465	40,585	38,522	30,737	51,572
Private	63,042	47,293	40,010	36,674	31,254	48,852
Percentage of teacher education mean salary to all disciplines mean salary						
Public	87.1	91.9	93.4	91.1	100.1	86.9
Private	87.2	91.9	90.5	94.8	98.8	86.6

Source. College and University Personnel Association, published in *Chronicle of Higher Education* (April 4, 1997).

exception of social work at research institutions, education programs generate a much greater percentage of GSCH than the other professional programs (Howard et al., 1998).

COMPARISON OF SALARIES IN EDUCATION COLLEGES, SCHOOLS, AND DEPARTMENTS

Mean salaries for the 1996-1997 academic year for teacher education faculty were compared with the mean salaries of faculty from all disciplines by rank and total. As illustrated in Table 1, it is clear that teacher education faculties, on average, are paid less than the average salary of faculty at U.S. colleges and universities. Specifically, during that academic year, over all ranks, the average salary paid to a teacher education faculty member was about 13% below the average. Given that most salary increases are a percentage of the previous year's salary, it can be assumed that this discrepancy is even larger today.

Another comparative index of expenditures in education to other disciplines is that of administrative salaries, specifically the salaries paid to

Table 2
Median Salaries of Selected Academic Deans by Institutional Category for 1998-1999 ($)

Discipline	All	Doctoral	Comprehensive	Baccalaureate
Architecture	114,637	123,670	92,700	
Agriculture	113,739	142,588	83,500	
Arts and sciences	91,796	130,010	89,484	67,610
Business	92,833	144,244	96,614	60,000
Education	89,300	118,024	84,797	56,000
Engineering	128,372	149,031	102,500	76,017
Fine arts	85,431	111,254	88,000	57,866
Law	164,347	170,514	163,000	57,866
Pharmacy	133,672	136,500	112,516	
Social work	101,000	122,000	80,018	41,035
Nursing	82,154	124,042	82,680	58,918
Average	108,844	133,807	97,796	59,414

Source. College and University Personnel Association, published in *Chronicle of Higher Education* (March 5, 1999).

academic deans. Presented in Table 2 are the median salaries paid to deans in selected academic disciplines in 1998-1999. Comparison of the median salaries of the deans of colleges of education to the other median deans' salaries clearly indicates that senior education administrators are at the lowest or near the lowest of their counterparts' salary scale.

As personnel is the major expenditure of most education units (90% to 95% for most programs), the above salary comparisons support the validity of the findings of the comparison expenditures of education programs with other disciplines. These data indicate that the faculty and administrators who staff and teach in the education programs in colleges and universities across the nation, in general, are not compensated for their efforts at levels equal to that of their academic colleagues in other disciplines. In addition, these data indicate that the faculty and professional staff serving in most college and university education programs have only marginally adequate resources to support continuous professional development.

REALLOCATION OF RESOURCES WITHIN THE COLLEGE OR UNIVERSITY

If schools, colleges, and departments of education (SCDEs) are to receive more resources, there will have to be an infusion of new money from outside sources (most likely the state or federal government) or from the reallocation of resources within each institution. The possibility of new funding from the federal government for ongoing and long-term operations is not likely. Some states may choose to provide additional money to universities to produce more teachers, but the likelihood of states providing funds to increase the expenditures per SCH is small. State governments tend to emphasize quantity over quality, usually reacting to existing or projected statewide teacher shortages. As such, education deans, department heads, and faculty must look to their presidents and provosts for assistance in increasing the expenditures per SCH. But why would university and college presidents and provosts want to do that?

Quality

SCDE leaders will argue that an increase in expenditures per SCH is needed to ensure high-quality teacher education programs. A major problem with this argument, however, is the lack of consensus in the field of teacher education about what constitutes quality. The consensus about the definition of quality in most other professions is greater than that in education, as evidenced by the acceptance of accreditation. Other professional schools and programs such as engineering, nursing, medicine, law, and architecture rely on standards applied through national professional accreditation as the single accepted means to define their professions and what it takes to educate a high-quality professional. In most of the major professions, candidates must first graduate from an accredited university or college program before they can be considered for licensure. As a consequence, nearly all recognized professional programs in higher education are accredited through a recognized national professional accrediting body.

This is not the case in education. Many SCDEs (40% to 50% including some at major universities) still choose not to seek national accreditation through the National Council for Accreditation of Teacher Education, currently the only approved accrediting body for teacher education. A new effort to create a different accrediting body as described in the article by Frank Murray (2000 [this issue]) further undermines potential consensus in the field about what constitutes quality in teacher education. This lack of a national consensus weakens most arguments college and university education administrators make to their presidents or provosts regarding quality and the need for more funding per SCH. Teacher education deans or program chairs who urge their superiors to provide funding adequate to meet high accreditation standards are undermined when their presidents can site prestigious universities that have chosen to ignore the standards. Moreover, the accrediting body itself is weakened because it must be careful not to require standards that are too high for fear of losing university participants.

The history of the AACTE reveals a long and difficult battle between those who support national accreditation and those who oppose it. Richard Wisniewski, a past president of AACTE, summarizes the conflict in an e-mail message reported by Ducharme and Ducharme (1998):

During the year I struggled to get AACTE to link membership to NCATE accreditation, it was not clear until the final vote how large a chasm exists between those supporting and those opposed to national accreditation. The depth of feelings about the issues had never been as forcefully revealed. That we continue to debate the NCATE issue reveals the fundamental weakness of the teacher education enterprise. We are the only professional group that takes public pride in attacking a hallmark of every other profession, national accreditation. We preach high standards for everyone else but ourselves. (p. 37)

In other words, the incentive to meet national accreditation standards is not as great in teacher education programs as it would (and should) be if there were greater consensus among teacher educators and others in the profession about the benefits of high standards, defined through a single recognized national accrediting body. When every teacher candidate must first graduate from an accredited program before being considered for a teaching license, as recommended in *What Matters Most* (National Commission on Teaching & America's Future, 1996), education leaders on campuses of all types of higher education will be in much stronger positions to argue for greater expenditures per SCH. This is an important recommendation of one small group.

Investment

University presidents are logically willing to put money into programs that will bring a financial return to the campus. Multimillion-dollar grants with high indirect cost-return rates are very attractive, and departments that can obtain such grants are seen as worthy of investment. Grant money available for science, health, and agriculture is many times greater than that available in the field of education. To make matters worse, the indirect cost-return rate in those areas (grants funded by the National Science Foundation and the National Institutions of Health) is often much higher than those offered by the U.S. Department of Education. Consequently, deans and department chairs of SCDEs are not in a strong position to argue for more resources based on the notion that the increased resources would act as seed money, leading to large grants with good returns to the institution.

Gifts are another form of institutional income. Private colleges and universities have long depended on gifts from alumni, friends, and foundations to support their programs. This is becoming more and more the case for publicly supported postsecondary institutions. The common wisdom is that SCDEs have less potential to obtain large amounts of gift money because the alumni are teachers who make so little money. The recent $21 million gift to the School of Education at the University of Connecticut may be an indication that too many of us have underestimated the potential of SCDEs in that regard. Nevertheless, the perception, if not the reality, is that the potential of SCDEs for obtaining substantial gifts is not as great as in many other fields.

The other major sources of revenue for education programs and colleges are tuition and state funds. For private institutions, of course, only tuition applies. For purposes of this discussion, the two are the same. The basic principle is that SCH production equates to tuition money and, in most states, general fund support. In general, the more SCHs generated, the more tuition and general fund money comes to the campus. This is the one area in which SCDEs excel as areas of investment. SCDEs have the capacity to draw large numbers of students and thus SCH and money to the institution. The lower the expenditures per SCH, the more "profit" available for other initiatives and priorities across the campus.

SCDEs are a good investment for the university only insomuch as they generate inexpensive SCHs and lots of them. Other departments can argue that they bring large amounts of money into the college through gifts and grants. Still other departments can generate inexpensive SCHs through large sections of lower division classes. And, a few departments can do both. Education programs are disadvantaged by the fact that they usually offer few lower-division courses (typically less expensive than the institutional average) and high percentages of upper-division and/or graduate courses. In addition, these programs require of their students many hours of clinical experiences (all typically more expensive than the university average). One would expect that the expenditures per SCH would be greater in SCDEs than in programs with many lower division courses and few graduate courses or clinical experiences.

In spite of this, and for SCDEs to be worthy of investment, they must generate large numbers of inexpensive SCHs or become financial burdens to the campuses. Financial burdens are tolerated on university and college campuses if they serve a valued community need (like nursing) and their standards are high.

So, we return to the importance of high standards and accreditation. SCDEs will continue to be in weak positions to negotiate or effectively compete on their campuses for higher expenditures per SCH until the education profession takes a strong and consistent stand on high standards, established and monitored through a single national professional accreditation body.

REFERENCES

American Association of Colleges for Teacher Education (AACTE). (1987). *Teaching teachers: Facts and figures*. Washington, DC: Author.

Bowen, H. R. (1980). *The costs of higher education: How much do colleges and universities spend per student and how much should they spend?* San Francisco: Jossey-Bass.

Ducharme, E. R., & Ducharme, M. K. (1998). *The American Association of Colleges for Teacher Education: A history*. Washington DC: American Association for Teacher Education.

Ebmeier, H., Twombly, S., & Teeter, D. J. (1991). The comparability and adequacy of financial support for schools of education. *Journal of Teacher Education, 42*(3), 226-235.

Hample, S. R. (1980). *Cost studies in higher education* (AIR Professional File No. 7). Tallahassee, FL: Association for Institutional Research.

Howard, R. D., Hitz, R., & Baker, L. (1997). *Comparative study of expenditures per student credit hour of education programs to programs of other disciplines and professions*. Report prepared for the Government Relations Committee of the American Association of Colleges for Teacher Education, the Association of Colleges and Schools of the Education in State Universities and Land Grant Colleges and Affiliated Private Universities, and the Teacher Education Council for State Colleges and Universities.

Howard, R. D., Hitz, R., & Baker, L. (1998). A national study comparing the expenditures of teacher education programs by Carnegie classification and with other disciplines. *Action in Teacher Education, 20*(3), 1-14.

Murray, F. B. (2000). The role of accreditation reform in teacher education. *Educational Policy, 14*(1), 40-59.

National Commission on Teaching & America's Future. (1996). *What matters most: Teaching for America's future*. New York: Author.

Office of Institutional Research and Planning. (1996). *Summary report refined means for workload, cost, and productivity indicators, by CIP code and Carnegie classification*. University of Delaware: Author.

Walters, D. L. (1981). *Financial analysis for academic units* (AAHE_ERIC/Higher Education Research Report No. 7). Washington, DC: American Association for Higher Education.

Part 5

The Final Arena: Building
Capacity for Change

Afterword

Teaching for America's Future: National Commissions and Vested Interests in an Almost Profession

LINDA DARLING-HAMMOND

This article describes how the National Commission on Teaching has sought to implement its recommendations by working with partner states, districts, and stakeholder organizations that are committed to improving the quality of teaching. By creating a comprehensive agenda, democratizing the process of reform, and developing collaborative partnerships, the commission has stimulated substantial ongoing reform in policy and practice. As in the professionalization of medicine, law, and other fields, the creation of a professional accountability system for preparation and practice is a critical next step. If all teachers are to have access to knowledge and all students are to have access to well-prepared teachers, universities and schools will need to develop new partnerships and joint commitments to a democratic profession of teaching based on shared accountability for teacher education.

IN THE OPENING ARTICLE of this issue, Karen Gallagher and Jerry Bailey ask whether the work of the National Commission on Teaching and America's Future (NCTAF) should be dismissed with that of other commissions that have made pronouncements and disappeared or whether it may ultimately have greater impact because of the systemic scope of its recommendations, their strong research grounding, and the commission's work with partner organizations, states, and districts in the 3 years since its report, *What*

EDUCATIONAL POLICY, Vol. 14 No. 1, January and March 2000 162-183
© 2000 Corwin Press, Inc.

Matters Most (1996), was released. An equally important question is whether the commission's major goal—a caring, competent, and qualified teaching force for all children in all communities—has a chance of being realized in our lifetimes. If the goal is achieved, it will be through the efforts of the thousands of educators, policy makers, and others involved in this work. If it is not, the creation of a deeply divided society, fueled largely by starkly differential access to high-quality teaching for the more and less advantaged members of our nation, could endanger our democracy.

In this article, I suggest that, although the commission has had an effect far beyond its members' boldest imaginations and substantially greater than most other such bodies, there are several key battles not yet won that will make the difference between localized changes that benefit only some communities and widespread changes that influence the system as a whole. These systemwide changes are those needed to address the key equity issues that threaten increasingly to create an underclass of citizens who have no chance of participating effectively in a knowledge-based society. It is largely because these changes directly confront the allocation of opportunity in the society as a whole that they are so hard fought and their politics are so intense.

In what follows, I describe the commission's work and many of its impacts over the past 3 years, how it has achieved these outcomes, what major political battles it faces, what professional and public interests are at stake, and what I believe will need to happen to make good on the promise that should be every child's educational birthright: a caring, competent teacher in every classroom.

COMMISSIONS AND POLITICAL CHANGE

Given our society's rapidly changing goals for education—and increasingly common perceptions that the education system must be redesigned to achieve these goals—it is not surprising that we have experienced nearly two decades' worth of commission reports at the federal, state, and local levels. Commissions are a common response to a felt need for change. In times of perceived crisis, commission reports are important vehicles for defining the problem and hence for deciding in what arenas solutions will be sought. This important function can mobilize energies in helpful directions. As new policies are forged to meet perceived problems or needs, the definition of the problem is critical to the appropriate identification of potential solutions and strategies.

Of course, commissions are not always helpful. If the source of the problem is misdiagnosed, follow-up efforts will be misdirected and will have limited potential to actually improve the situation that has given rise to concern.

Even elegant statements of the problem and well-conceived solutions may have little effect if they are not linked to on-the-ground mobilization of efforts that bring information and people together in the practical pursuit of change. Thus, many commission reports are greeted with a moment of media fanfare and quickly fade away into oblivion, gathering dust on academics' shelves.

On the other hand, commission reports have the capacity to point the attention of a broad range of constituents to new areas of work that, if well conceived, can make a different in public policy. They can help to galvanize support from practitioners, policy makers, and the public for broad changes in the systems that influence teaching and learning. Particularly in our complex, decentralized education system in which simultaneous efforts are required from so many different sectors and institutions, a coordinated strategy that links policy and practice—and that links changes in schools with changes in the teaching profession—is essential to the lasting success of any reform initiatives. This is what the NCTAF has sought to do, not only in its report but also in its follow-up work.

As Gallagher and Bailey (2000a [this issue]) suggest, the commission did at least three things that set it apart from many other such bodies:

- It created a comprehensive, interlocking agenda and outlined how it could be achieved through specific, joint efforts of many actors rather than identifying a single, simple panacea that, even if implemented, would be bound, by itself, to fail;
- It sought to democratize the process of reform by actively involving a range of stakeholders at the local and state levels in evaluating their own needs and developing their own strategies for reform rather than relying on the pronouncements of far-away elites as the primary lever for change; and
- It developed collaborative partnerships for work on shared agendas of concern, reaching out to the field and helping others secure resources to take on the work, advancing the NCTAF agenda by handing it away.

NCTAF's effort to democratize the process of change and to engage a wide range of stakeholders in the agenda have probably been critical to its success thus far.

IMPACTS OF THE COMMISSION'S WORK

In just 3 years, the commission has changed much of the policy conversation about education reform in the United States. Although concerns about teaching and teacher education were raised in earlier reports like the Holmes

Group's (1986) *Tomorrow's Teachers* and the Carnegie Task Force's (1986) *A Nation Prepared*, the discourse about change was largely limited to the profession, with little spillover to the general public or the policy community. The standards-based reform movement launched in the early 1990s focused primarily on issues of curriculum and testing, with little recognition of the critical role of teaching in what happens in classrooms. Media discussions of education included lots of hand-wringing about declining test scores but little attention to instruction.

What Matters Most (NCTAF, 1996) and the commission's subsequent work have stimulated more than 1,500 news articles and editorials nationally and abroad, hundreds of pieces of state and federal legislation, a wide array of local initiatives to improve teaching, and at least two federally funded research and development initiatives both explicitly organized around the commission's agenda—the National Center for the Study of Teaching and Policy and the National Partnership for Excellence and Accountability in Teaching—that bring together researchers, professional associations, policy makers, and practitioners to enhance knowledge and practice in the fields of teaching and policy.

When it was released, President Clinton endorsed *What Matters Most* (NCTAF, 1996) and issued a directive to the secretary of education to support states and localities in responding to the report's recommendations. The directive reiterated the commission's major message, stating, "Every child needs—and deserves—dedicated, outstanding teachers, who know their subject matter, are effectively trained, and know how to teach to high standards and to make learning come alive for students." Also on the day of the report's release, the Department of Education issued an initial response to the recommendations of the commission, outlining steps the department could take to address each recommendation. In a February 1997 address at the State Department, First Lady Hillary Rodham Clinton alluded to the president's directive, saying that the president had "called on the National Commission on Teaching and America's Future for a new effort to help communities and states promote excellence and accountability in teaching." In June 1997, the department released a widely disseminated report titled *Excellence and Accountability in Teaching: A Guide to US Department of Education Programs and Resources* in response to the president's directive. An update was released in 1998, as the department has continued to encourage and track teaching quality initiatives.

The president's budget for fiscal year 1998 called for major investments in teacher training, including funding for 100,000 teachers to seek national board certification. Many of the commission's findings and recommendations were reflected in federal legislative proposals in the 105th Congress that ultimately comprised the components of Title V of the Higher Education Reauthorization Act. Most of the bills cited the commission report directly, and statistics from the commission's report were often used to define the problem. The administration's bill noted,

The National Commission on Teaching and America's Future found that 50,000 uncertified individuals annually enter teaching because schools, frequently those in urban and rural areas with large concentrations of children from low-income families, cannot find all the certified teachers they need.

George Miller's (D-CA) Teaching Excellence for All Children Act (H.R. 2228) framed the need for more qualified teachers with this finding: "The National Commission on Teaching and America's Future has found that one quarter of the nation's classroom teachers are not fully qualified to teach in their subject areas."

New legislation in the 1999 Congress has also returned to the commission's work. Legislation to improve teacher education, invest in teacher recruitment, and support stronger professional development is being developed both as part of other major reauthorizations (e.g., the Elementary and Secondary Education Act) and in new legislation. Here, too, *What Matters Most* is a touch point for defining the problems of ad hoc recruitment, inadequate training for many, and drive-by workshops in lieu of sustained professional development. The report is also often used to frame the solutions. This is, however, a more knotty problem, as Earley's article (2000 [this issue]) suggests and as I discuss further below.

More important than the national-level attention to the commission's work has been a widespread policy effort at the state level where most education policy is made. Immediately after the release of the report, 12 states joined the commission as partners, working collaboratively with the support of their governors, state education departments, legislative leaders, and education leaders to develop strategies for implementing the commission's recommendations. Since then, 3 additional states have become partners. The group of 15 state partners now includes Alabama, Georgia, Idaho, Illinois, Indiana, Kansas, Kentucky, Maine, Maryland, Missouri, Montana, North Carolina, Ohio, Oklahoma, and Washington. Each state partner established a policy group of key stakeholders, including state officials from all branches of government, education leaders in K-12 and higher education, and members of the public representing business, parents, community organizations, and others. This group oversaw the conduct of a data-based policy inventory to evaluate the condition of teaching and teacher education in the state. The inventory, organized around the commission's five major recommendations (see Gallagher & Bailey, 2000a), is the basis for a state strategic plan crafted by the policy group to guide policy and program development for developing a high-quality teaching force. A considerable amount of reform consistent with the commission's recommendations has taken place in all of the commission's partner states. North Carolina, for instance, passed the ambitious Excellent Schools Act of 1997, which enacted nearly all the commission's recommendations that were not already in place. The bill increases salaries, strengthens licensing, establishes rewards for knowledge and skills, improves teacher education, enhances mentoring of beginning teachers, and funds professional development tied to student standards. Ohio's state board and legislature have enacted policies that adopt performance-based standards for teacher licensing, require teacher education programs to meet National Council for Accreditation of Teacher Education (NCATE) standards, provide mentors for all beginning teachers and principals, require license renewal every 5 years, require a master's degree or the equivalent, support national board certification, and encourage peer review and assistance. Indiana has also moved to a performance-based assessment system of accreditation, certification, and licensure and is building a similarly comprehensive plan (Scannell & Metcalf, 2000 [this issue]).

Maryland and Georgia have made substantial comprehensive progress in the pursuit of the teaching quality reform agenda through their P-16 councils. These councils have developed a strong, inclusive group of stakeholders and an organizational infrastructure to guide education reform. As Kettlewell, Kaste, and Jones (2000 [this issue]) report, the use of standards to guide co-reform of schools and teacher education has been a linchpin for change in Georgia. In addition, a partnership supported by the national commission between the Council for Basic Education and the American Association of Colleges for Teacher Education (AACTE) has worked directly with teacher preparation programs on strengthening and connecting training in content and content pedagogy around the new standards.

Many nonpartner states, too, have undertaken reform initiatives in support of higher quality teaching. Arkansas, for example, used the commission's report as a basis for 1996 legislation raising teacher salaries and improving benefits, creating supports for national board certification, and increasing teacher planning time. Connecticut developed new performance-based licensing rules, became a partner with NCATE, and expanded requirements for in-service professional development. And South Carolina raised teachers' salaries, enacted incentives for national board certification, and charged the state board with upgrading teacher education standards, enacting tests for licensure, and developing an induction program for beginning teachers.

One region organized a coordinated regional response to *What Matters Most* (NCTAF, 1996): In November 1997, the Columbia Group, a consortium of business-supported public policy centers in the six southeast states, issued a report titled *Teachers and Teaching in the Southeast*, which examines the status of teaching in the region. The Columbia Group issued its report as part of its ongoing efforts to advance the commission's work. With the support of key organizations in these states and a local foundation, the commission established a southeastern regional office that is working intensely on research and development related to investments in teaching quality.

In July 1997, the commission launched an urban initiative that is developing a network of school districts committed to improving their teacher development systems. The commission provides districts with technical assistance for analyzing needs and mobilizing changes in teacher recruitment, preparation, hiring, induction, reward, support, and professional development practices; documents and disseminates information about successful strategies and practices; and provides networking resources for groups that rarely have opportunities to learn from one another. Partner districts include Albuquerque, New Mexico; Birmingham, Alabama; Cincinnati, Ohio; New York City; San Antonio, Texas; San Diego, California; Seattle, Washington; and Stamford, Connecticut. Through the Teacher Union Reform Network (TURN), a group of reform-minded teacher union locals from both the National Education Association (NEA) and the American Federation of Teachers (AFT), the commission works with several other districts, including Rochester and Syracuse, New York; Hammond, Indiana; Columbus and Toledo, Ohio; Minneapolis, Minnesota; and Los Angeles.

HOW THE COMMISSION HAS ENCOURAGED ON-THE-GROUND REFORM

The commission's widespread impact may be partly attributable to timing. In an election year in which the U.S. public targeted education as its number one concern (*USA Today*/CNN Gallup Poll, 1996) and ranked "good teachers" as the most important thing schools need to do a good job (Johnson & Immerwahr, 1994), it may be that the message found the most fertile ground available in years. In addition, the report benefited from the accumulation over the past decade of a much sturdier body of research on teaching, teacher development, school reforms, and policy effects than was once available to support the ruminations of bodies such as this.

Rather than merely identify the problems and make general recommendations about solutions, the commission grounded each of its recommendations in real-world examples of programs and practices that have evidence of effectiveness. In addition, since *What Matters Most* was released, the commission has continued to conduct and disseminate research on highly effective policies and practices so that others can learn from successful strategies. In addition to case studies of seven exemplary teacher education programs, the commission has published case studies on the successful school recruitment and teacher development strategies in New Haven, California, and the highly effective, systemic approach to professional development launched in School District #2 in New York City. Additional case studies of Rochester, New York's, extraordinary teacher evaluation plan; Albuquerque, New Mexico's successful teacher induction model; Cincinnati, Ohio's, comprehensive approach to teacher preparation and development; and successful state policy strategies for reforming licensing, preparation, compensation, and professional development in North Carolina, Connecticut, and Ohio also provide user-friendly research that can inform local, state, and regional policy work.

There are other reasons that public interest has been sustained well beyond the initial burst of press coverage 3 years ago. One is the continual provision of information to the media and stakeholders concerned with these issues. The commission has learned to disseminate information to policy and program developers in ways that are much more effective than publishing articles only in research journals or sending out reports in brown paper wrappers. Commission staff have viewed media work as an educative process, not just a matter of getting coverage, and have worked to educate large segments of the general and professional media about teacher quality issues so that they develop more informed and constant reporting about teaching.

The commission's press conferences and later reports documenting programs that work have provided grist for extensive media coverage of teacher quality issues. In 1996, editorials and articles about the commission's report ran in all the major national newspapers from the *New York Times* and *Washington Post* to the *Los Angeles Times* and *Chicago Tribune*, while hundreds of newspapers across the country endorsed its recommendations. The report's state-by-state report card, providing statistics about teacher quality variables on a state basis, was a powerful news hook that made the issue more salient to local reporters and audiences. Major broadcast networks, news services, and cable networks carried stories about the report and have continued to follow up on teacher quality concerns regularly over the past 3 years. For the first time in decades, back-to-school stories in 1996 and each year since have focused on issues of teaching rather than emphasizing issues like discipline, uniforms, facilities, and sports.

The education press has been even more intensely engaged with these issues. In addition to running several front-page articles about the commission over the past 3 years, *Education Week* launched an essay series titled "What Matters Most: Essays on Teaching & America's Future," dealing with the issues of teacher quality and teacher preparation raised by the commission's report. The newspaper also published a series titled "What Matters Most: Strategies for Effective Teaching," which featured articles about the Interstate New Teacher Assessment and Support Consortium (INTASC), professional standards boards, teacher hiring practices, NCATE, school staffing, and Cincinnati's holistic approach to teacher preparation.

Much of the commission staff's dissemination work taps into existing dissemination mechanisms in the education community. Professional journals like *Education Leadership, Phi Delta Kappan, Journal of Staff Development*, and many organizations' newsletters have devoted articles and even whole issues to the teacher quality agenda and the commission's work. Many organizations have focused their own reform efforts on the commission's recommendations. A number of national professional associations have passed resolutions endorsing the commission's recommendations. Many others have engaged in support activities ranging from posting the commission's documents on their Web sites, publishing newsletter and journal articles, and holding conference sessions about the report to copublishing how-to handbooks and participating in research and implementation partnerships with the commission.

Professional associations also have adopted policy actions consistent with the commission's recommendations. In 1997, for example, the membership of the NEA endorsed the principle of peer review and the Association of Teacher Educators launched a standards-setting initiative for college faculty who prepare prospective teachers. The NEA and the AFT held a joint national conference on teaching quality in September 1998. Several partner states—including Kansas, North Carolina, Indiana, Idaho, Illinois, and Ohio—have held large statewide conferences to encourage broad-based public engagement.

A second reason for the ongoing extensive work on this agenda has been the commission's development of partnerships with a wide range of stakeholders engaged in research and reform. The commission staff does not have the capacity to lead all of the necessary efforts within the policy maker, practitioner, and public communities, nor does it want to do so. Instead, the key to sustained momentum on these issues lies in the commission's ability to infuse its ideals, ideas, knowledge base, and actions in the work of other educational policy organizations, professional associations, research institutes, and business and community groups.

The commission's approach to technical assistance is to provide help and leadership to prospective leaders of the teaching quality reform agenda and to forge partnerships with a wide range of stakeholders who can carry on the work in a variety of ways. For example, the National Governors Association and the National Conference on State Legislatures have worked with the commission and with each other on supporting the teacher quality agenda. With these and other partners, NCTAF has copublished reports about policy and program models and disseminated research findings to their members through their organizational vehicles—newsletters, magazines, conferences, and board meetings. These efforts help many audiences understand the interlocking recommendations developed by the commission and encourage activities toward reform from many vantage points. The staff of policy and professional organizations have grown increasingly knowledgeable about teacher policies and programs, thus increasing the capacity of their own organizations to be effective change agents.

The commission has also helped to broker relationships among parts of the system that do not normally work together—helping to create partnerships for change between administrators and teachers' organizations, for example, among school boards and legislators, and among governors, legislators, and higher education organizations. At the state and local levels, staff members have worked to develop cross-sector policy groups that do the work of public engagement and consensus building locally, using the knowledge about successful program models and policy strategies that NCTAF and others are able to provide to them. The commission has helped encourage and raise funds for many new professional collaborations that advance the work on the ground. NCTAF is currently involved with collaborative projects involving more than 20 different professional and policy organizations that are working on teacher quality concerns. The increased capacity of these organizations to work together around a common agenda with shared information has mobilized much more change than would have been possible had the small staff of the commission used its energies to try to respond one on one to requests for assistance from school districts and schools.

The articles in this issue about on-the-ground reforms in Indiana, Georgia, Cincinnati, and the University of Kansas provide evidence about how the change process actually works. All of them emphasize the importance of partnerships and collaboration guided by professional standards and a systemic vision. They illustrate how real change is a product of commitment that combines internal determination with external forces that leverage reform across constituencies and keep it pointed toward meaningful goals. They also illustrate how difficult the change process is and, by inference, how easy it can be in many places to lose track of what matters most as politics converge or collide with institutional self-interests. When this occurs, the rhetoric of reform can be hijacked by the sirens of the status quo. As I discuss below, this is happening in many venues as the real meaning of reform for vested interests becomes clear.

Although there is certainly a lot of productive policy and program work under way across the country, legislators and implementers do not always understand how to secure the outcomes they seek. For example, as states enact beginning teacher induction programs as recommended by the commission, they also need to take into account how to provide well-trained mentors and adequate guidance for mentoring. As states look for ways of expanding the pool of prospective teachers, they need to understand how to construct pathways for midcareer entrants that provide high-quality preparation for a successful teaching career rather than allowing minimally trained teachers to be hired without providing any safeguards for children. In too many cases, the importance of subject matter and teaching knowledge to teachers' effectiveness is overlooked. The pursuit of "alternatives" often means the continuation of the status quo—that is, the provision of underprepared teachers to the children of the poor. Although legislation is always partial and imperfect, it is important to develop greater understanding of the strategies that are likely actually to work in the long run to ensure higher quality teaching for all children.

At this stage in the work, it is of primary importance that advocates of teaching quality support greater knowledge among policy makers and education leaders about the factors that influence teachers' effectiveness, so that reforms do not devolve into simplistic and ineffectual silver bullets. It is an ongoing challenge to help change agents understand how to promote more coherent systemic policies and practices that consistently embrace the goals of quality teaching. This means that the commission and its associates must be even more strategic in continuing to further develop alliances, especially with organizations that heretofore have not fully understood, valued, or maintained a consistent focus on the teaching quality agenda.

CHASING THE DRAGON:
THE CURRENT BACKLASH

It is perhaps a testament to the power of the commission's agenda and the constituencies it has mobilized that a well-funded, right-wing backlash has formed against the commission, against university-based teacher education, and against national standards for teacher licensing, certification, and accreditation. Led by the Heritage Foundation, the Pioneer Institute, and, more recently, by Chester Finn's family-funded Fordham Foundation, the most vocal cheerleaders for the continuation of the status quo argue against teaching standards and teacher education investments on several grounds (Fordham Foundation, 1999, quoted in *Education Daily*):

- teacher training programs have "very low entry requirements, no exit requirements, scant subject content and a surfeit of pedagogical courses of uncertain value";
- teacher certification (i.e., licensing) "is not an effective quality control mechanism, but it is part of the regulatory mindset," whereas alternative certification routes promise to help schools recruit better instructors from a wider array of backgrounds;
- national accreditation through NCATE is "more concerned with a school's philosophical perspective than with the qualifications of its faculty and the knowledge of its graduates"; and
- the National Board for Professional Teaching Standards, which certifies accomplished teachers, uses "flawed" standards and assessments that bear no relation to student outcomes.

This attack on professional standards cuts to the center of the commission's (NCTAF, 1996) recommendations, based on a belief that

Standards for teaching are the linchpin for transforming current systems of preparation, licensing, certification, and ongoing development so that they better support student learning. [Such standards] can bring clarity and focus to a set of activities that are currently poorly connected and often badly organized. . . . Clearly, if students are to achieve high standards, we can expect no less from their teachers and from other educators. (p. 67)

At the heart of this argument are the ideas that professional standards are a lever for raising the quality of practice and that they are central to the cause of equity, protecting especially the least advantaged clientele from unscrupulous or incompetent practitioners. Standard setting is at the heart of every profession. When people seek help from doctors, lawyers, accountants, engineers, or architects, they rely on the unseen work of a three-legged stool supporting professional competence: accreditation, licensing, and certification. In virtually all professions other than teaching, candidates must graduate from an accredited professional school that provides up-to-date knowledge and systematic training to sit for the state licensing examinations that test their knowledge and skill. The accreditation process is meant to ensure that all preparation programs provide a reasonably common body of knowledge and structured training experiences that are comprehensive and up to date.

Licensing examinations, developed by members of the profession through state professional standards boards, are meant to ensure that candidates have acquired the knowledge they need to practice responsibly. The tests generally include both surveys of specialized information and performance components that examine aspects of applied practice in the field: Lawyers must analyze cases and develop briefs or memoranda of law to address specific issues, doctors must diagnose patients via case histories and describe the treatments they would prescribe, and engineers must demonstrate that they can apply certain principles to particular design situations.

In addition, many professions offer additional examinations that provide recognition for advanced levels of skill, such as certification for public accountants, board certification for doctors, and registration for architects. The certification standards are used not only to designate higher levels of competence but also to ensure that professional schools incorporate new knowledge into their courses and that practitioners incorporate such knowledge in their practice. They also guide professional development and evaluation throughout the career. Thus, these advanced standards may be viewed as the engine that pulls along the knowledge base of the profession. Together, standards for accreditation, licensing, and certification support quality assurance and ensure that new knowledge will be incorporated into training and used in practice.

Until recently, teaching has not had a coherent set of standards created by the profession to guide education, entry into the field, and ongoing practice. In the past 10 years, such standards have been created by NCATE, which sets standards for schools of education; INTASC, a group of more than 30 states working to develop standards for the licensing of beginning teachers; and the National Board for Professional Teaching Standards, which sets standards for accomplished practice and offers advanced certificates. These standards are aligned with one another and with new standards for student learning in the disciplines, they are based on the most current research on teaching and learning, and they are tied to performance-based assessments of teacher knowledge and skill. The standards see teaching as diagnostic: that is, as responsive to and contingent on student learning rather than the mere implementation of routines. The assessments look at evidence of teaching ability (videotapes of teaching, lesson plans, student work, analyses of curriculum) in the context of real teaching and in relation to evidence of student learning.

What do the standards require? The INTASC standards for teacher licensing spell out the competencies beginning teachers should have. These include the following:

- knowledge of subject matter and how to teach it to students;
- understanding of how to foster learning and development and how to address special learning needs;
- ability to assess students, plan curriculum, and use a range of teaching strategies that develop high levels of student performance;
- ability to create a positive, purposeful learning environment; and
- ability to collaborate with parents and colleagues to support student learning and to evaluate the effects of one's own teaching to continually improve it.

The NCATE standards require a teacher education program to

- offer a coherent program of studies based on a knowledge base about effective teaching,
- provide a full foundation in the liberal arts and in the discipline to be taught,
- prepare candidates to teach children so that they can achieve student learning standards in the disciplines,
- prepare teachers who can work with diverse learners and with new technologies, and
- ensure that candidates gain knowledge of effective learning and teaching strategies as described in the INTASC standards and demonstrate their skills in working with students.

The national board offers detailed standards in 30 areas, defined by subject area and developmental level of students, which reflect these five propositions:

- Teachers are committed to students and their learning. National-board-certified teachers are dedicated to ensuring their students' success. They understand how students develop and learn, and they adjust their practice based on student needs.
- Teachers know the subjects they teach and how to teach those subjects to students. Teachers use their deep understanding of subject matter to make it accessible to students.
- Teachers are responsible for managing and monitoring student learning. Teachers use their range of instructional techniques when each is appropriate. They know how to motivate and engage students, assess their learning, and explain student performance to parents.

- Teachers think systematically about their practice and learn from experience. National-board-certified teachers critically examine their practice, seek advice from others, and use research to improve their teaching.
- Teachers are members of learning communities. They work collaboratively with parents and other professionals on behalf of students.

To support their belief that quality will result from deregulation alone, the advocates for a free-market approach to teacher hiring and teacher education ignore the extensive evidence demonstrating the significant effects of teacher education and certification on student learning (for a recent review, see Darling-Hammond, 1999), the extensive body of research on teaching incorporated into NCATE's and INTASC's standards, and the decade's worth of research underlying the national board's standards and assessments. Unfortunately, all the evidence that currently exists suggests that the end result of their arguments will be the continuation of the grossly unequal system we currently operate, in which the profession has few means for infusing knowledge into preparation and training; meanwhile, the schools that serve the most advantaged students insist on well-trained teachers, whereas those that serve poor and minority students will get what is left over from a system that has no engine for quality and no basis for distributing it equitably.

The Fordham Foundation also has developed a teacher quality manifesto, which proposes that school administrators should make all teacher hiring and evaluation decisions (without interference from licensing agencies or central offices) provided that they assess instructors' skills by measuring student performance (*Education Daily*, April 22, 1999). The end result of this approach will be even less incentive than currently exists in the system for teachers to choose to teach the students who have the most difficulty learning, leaving these students with even fewer avenues to secure good teaching. Coupled with ongoing resistance to school funding equalization and support for policies that will set promotions and graduation on the basis of test scores, the far right's approach to reform is likely to result in even lower quality instruction for the children of the poor and disenfranchisement of many who have special learning needs, as schools seek to raise their average test scores by keeping low-scoring students back or pushing them out entirely. (For evidence on these outcomes of test-based accountability schemes, see Allington & McGill-Franzen, 1992; Orfield & Ashkinaze, 1991; Smith, 1986.)

Is the argument for professional standards as a top-down regulatory approach at odds with decentralized performance-driven reforms, as Finn and colleagues argue? We believe it is not. Far from usurping the authority of parents and community members, teaching standards can help ensure that all students have teachers who are better equipped to work with and support students and families. This should ultimately promote many different models of education, because many regulations that currently constrain schools will be unnecessary if the state takes care of its key obligation: the preparation and equitable distribution of highly qualified teachers who know how to do their jobs well. If policy makers and the public are convinced that educators are well prepared to make sound decisions, they should find it less necessary to regulate schools against the prospect of incompetence. Assuring quality in the teaching force is, we believe, actually the best way to support decentralization and local control in education.

The Accreditation Wars

Like the Fordham Foundation, Frank Murray (2000 [this issue]) argues against professional standards on the grounds that they are meaningless; in this case, he argues that there is not enough research on teaching to adopt standards of practice. He contradicts himself with his own statements about what "we know" about the nature of learning (statements made with great certitude about a knowledge base he has just disclaimed). He also contradicts himself by suggesting, on one hand, that his Teacher Education Accreditation Council (TEAC) will accredit schools of education against their own internally derived goals and standards and, later on, by claiming that the standards TEAC uses will be compatible with those of NCATE.

It is puzzling to imagine what "accreditation" could mean in the TEAC context. Professional accreditation as it is commonly understood means that an enterprise has met standards established by the profession as determined by a process enforced by the profession. TEAC was formed by an organization of college presidents and includes no organizational representation from any of the 30 professional associations of teachers, administrators, teacher educators, or the representatives of parents, community members, and policy makers who comprise the governing body of NCATE. As TEAC has presented its plans, it does not intend to include organizations representing teachers and their standard-setting agencies in its governance structure; nor has it formally adopted any professional standards or professional review of programs as part of its review process. TEAC has not presented any standards that it will adhere to or enforce and has not articulated how it will know that a program has met any standards. It has not described the nature of the evidence it will require or what it will take to be persuaded that a program has satisfied its claims. Rhetoric about caring and competent teachers cannot substitute for professional standards. If TEAC represents itself as an accrediting body, having rejected professional standard setting in favor of each institution setting its own standards, it will lead the public to believe that institutions have met standards they do not meet. At best, this is disingenuous; at worst, it could be viewed as a form of consumer fraud.

There is more at stake here than the turf battles of warring organizations. As the move for professional standards has become stronger, as NCATE's own standards have become more rigorous, and as more than 40 states have entered partnerships with NCATE, the continuation of teacher education as a low-status, low-expenditure operation that provides revenues for other parts of the university could be threatened. The continuation of teaching as an enterprise in which low salaries are maintained by easy access and low standards might also be unsettled. Finally, the continuation of unequal funding schemes supported by lack of state responsibility to adhere to standards of care for all students might be unraveled if standards of teacher preparation and licensing were as strong as those in medicine, law, or other professions.

Because teacher education accreditation is voluntary in most states, some programs that are unaccredited would likely have little difficulty meeting the NCATE standards but have had no incentive for pursuing accreditation. Many others would not meet the standards because the content, coherence, and resources of their programs are inadequate. Studies indicating that negative NCATE reviews have led to substantial changes and investments in weak education programs (for example, Altenbaugh & Underwood, 1990) also highlight the fact that professional accreditation can be at odds with universities' desires to use education schools as "cash cows" for other parts of the university. (See Howard, Hitz, & Baker, 2000 [this issue], for evidence that schools of education continue to be less well funded than other professional programs.)

In their article on strategic philanthropy, Gallagher and Bailey (2000b [this issue]) describe how the professionalization of medicine depended on efforts of the American Medical Association's Council on Medical Education in supporting Abraham Flexner's research, establishing a system of accreditation, and encouraging states not to grant licenses to graduates of poorly rated schools. The American Bar Association undertook similar efforts to upgrade the quality of law schools in the early part of the century. In these and other professions, the insistence on mandatory accreditation of training institutions was a primary means of raising standards, infusing common knowledge into professional schools, and ensuring that all entrants got access to this knowledge.

There is no doubt that variability in quality is as great among teacher training programs as it once was among medical and law schools. The proprietary schools that provided quick routes into law and medicine at the turn of the century resemble the "summer wonder" programs like Teach for America and alternative certification routes in New Jersey and Texas that provide only a few weeks of training before allowing individuals to practice on children. Even within university-based programs, the range is wide. As one indication of the gap between program practices and professional standards, the initial failure rate for programs seeking accreditation in the 3 years after NCATE strengthened its standards in 1987 was 27%. During the first 3 years of implementation, almost half of the schools reviewed could not pass the new "knowledge base" standard, which specified that schools must be able to describe the knowledge base on which their programs rest. Most of these schools made major changes in their programs since that time, garnering new resources, making personnel changes, and revamping curriculum, and were successful in their second attempt at accreditation.

More than 90% of all programs that have stood for accreditation in the past several years report that the process led to major improvements in the quality of their programs. Interestingly, although Murray (2000) questions the utility of standards, the cases in this issue describing reforms in Georgia and Indiana and at the University of Cincinnati attest to the generative power of these standards in leveraging change. In addition, a recent analysis by the commission shows that the proportion of accredited schools of education in a state is the best predictor of the proportion of well-qualified teachers in that state (defined as the proportion holding full certification and a major in the field they teach), which, in turn, is by far the strongest predictor of student achievement on the National Assessment of Educational Progress (Darling-Hammond, 1999). Accreditation is one of the key levers that pushes a profession ahead and provokes real change.

NCATE upgraded its standards again in 1995 to incorporate the INTASC and national board standards, and it has even more ambitious plans for performance-based accreditation by the year 2000 (discussed later). This means that many programs that want to secure or maintain professional accreditation will need to upgrade their efforts further. There are unresolved financial, political, and substantive issues that will determine how many programs undertake these efforts.

Like the organizations of practicing doctors and lawyers that enforced standards for medical schools, organizations of practicing teachers ranging from the subject matter associations like the National Councils of Teachers of Mathematics and English to the NEA and the AFT favor national accreditation. However, universities that profit from teacher education are divided on the topic—as are colleges of education themselves. TEAC is only one of the obstacles to the process of ensuring greater accountability for what teachers know and can be expected to do. Founded by small liberal arts colleges fearful that their programs might not pass professional standards, TEAC may give protection to those that are unwilling to make the investments necessary to create high-quality teacher education programs; would prefer not to be held to uncomfortable expectations regarding the coherence of the courses they offer, the quality of the supervision they provide, or the diversity of their faculties and student bodies; and would like to preserve the illusion that they nonetheless meet professional standards by creating a way to say they are accredited by virtue of having met their own goals. TEAC's greatest success may be to preserve the subordinate position of teacher education in universities that do not want to support it financially or intellectually.

In the debates over the Federal Higher Education Act (Earley, 2000), the divisions within the teacher education community (the American Association of Colleges for Teacher Education, for example, lobbied against a provision to encourage accreditation as a means of accountability) ultimately contributed to the heavy-handed imposition of governmental accountability measures based on tests that bear little relation to teaching that are now a source of concern. Even more damaging to children was the education establishment's inability or unwillingness to take on the issue of alternative certification, which was inserted into legislation originally intended to improve preparation and which instead legitimized funding to low-quality proprietary programs offering little training and less quality control for teachers who will teach low-income and minority children. Where professions resist self-regulation, government regulation—which is often less well informed in its understanding of the field—is bound to increase. The market mentality that Earley (2000) deplores has been fed by the unwillingness of the teacher education establishment to set and enforce its own standards, thereby leaving itself open to charges of flaccidity, lack of responsiveness to public needs, and the defense of monopoly status while protecting weak programs.

The Costs of Avoiding Professional Accountability

This circling of the higher education wagons could very well spell the demise of university-based teacher education and of the professionalization of teaching. Thiessen (2000 [this issue]) describes how lack of confidence in weak teacher education programs in Great Britain caused so much government intervention that the enterprise of university-based teacher education has been almost undone intellectually. "Teacher training," he notes, "has become painting by numbers."

Rather than fending off the field as TEAC would do, divorcing academe from practitioners and from the world of practice, teacher educators need to become part of a responsible profession by embracing their partners in the arts and sciences and in the field. The University of Cincinnati (Mitchell, Castenell, Hendricks-Lee, & Mooney, 2000 [this issue]; Yinger & Hendricks-Lee, 2000 [this issue]) provides one model of the "joint academic-community definitions of problems, strategies, and definitions of success," Thiessen (2000) urges. The University of Kansas's collaborative approach to reform provides another (Mason, 2000 [this issue]). Although Murray (2000) characterizes as problematic the federal requirement that teacher educators collaborate with arts and sciences faculty and K-12 schools, Mason (2000) talks about the collaboration among these sectors as essential for the adequate preparation of teachers. Where Murray sees interlopers, Mason and her colleagues at the University of Kansas see the foundations of shared accountability.

The Real Stakes

If this were only an institutional question, few would care about the resolution of the issue. (And because many view it that way, those who should care often do not.) However, the ability of universities and schools to work together to educate teachers well is critical to the improvement of education, especially for the students who need good teaching most. If teachers and teacher educators do not act to develop a system of professional accountability that improves practice on a wide scale, greater governmental regulation of public institutions that constrains their ability to innovate and improve will continue even while other parts of the market are deregulated. Unregulated vouchers with few safeguards along with widened loopholes for entering teaching will likely jeopardize not only the educational welfare of the most vulnerable students, but also they may ultimately jeopardize the capacity of the system to operate well at all.

Although universities are essential to high-quality teacher education (Darling-Hammond, 1998; Mason, 2000; Thiessen, 2000; Yinger & Hendricks-Lee, 2000), universities cannot perform this function well alone. They must work with schools to create a more coherent and powerful form of preparation and with policy makers and public constituents to create a market for greater quality in both schools and universities. Universities cannot afford to circle the wagons and hide behind elite arguments against professional standards that loosen their connection to the field and to the new demands of schooling. Now, more than ever, they need to work to create a democratic profession of teaching.

Parents and the public have made it clear that they want well-qualified teachers (Recruiting New Teachers, 1998), and now they are paying greater attention to whether such teachers are being prepared, recruited, and retained in their local communities. This is the moment for teacher educators to join with public partners to press for reform. The articles in this issue demonstrate how collaborative efforts can get beyond narrowly conceived self-interests and make a difference in what happens for teachers and their students.

Although the path is difficult and outcomes are never guaranteed, continued engagement of all of the stakeholders in joint problem solving can make a difference in securing a caring, competent, and qualified teacher for every child.

REFERENCES

Allington, R. L., & McGill-Franzen, G. (1992). Unintended effects of educational reform. *Educational Policy, 6*(4): 397-414.

Altenbaugh, R. J., & Underwood, K. (1990). The evolution of normal schools. In J. I. Goodlad, R. Soder, & K. Sirotnik (Eds.), *Places where teachers are taught* (pp. 136-186). San Francisco: Jossey Bass.

Carnegie Task Force on the Teaching Profession. (1986). *A nation prepared: Teachers for the 21st century.* Washington, DC: Author.

Columbia Group. (1997, November). *Teachers and teaching in the Southeast.*

Darling-Hammond, L. (1998). The case for university-based teacher education. In R. Roth (Ed.), *The role of the university in the preparation of teachers* (pp. 13-30). Philadelphia: Falmer.

Darling-Hammond, L. (1999). *Teacher quality and student achievement: A review of state policy evidence.* Seattle: Center for the Study of Teaching and Policy, University of Washington.

Earley, P. M. (2000). Finding the culprit: Federal policy and teacher education. *Educational Policy, 14*(1), 25-39.

Fordham Foundation. (1999). *Better teachers, better schools.* Washington, DC: Author.

Gallagher, K. S., & Bailey, J. D. (2000a). Introduction to the politics of teacher preparation reform. *Educational Policy, 14*(1), 6-9.

Gallagher, K. S., & Bailey, J. D. (2000b). The politics of teacher education reform: Strategic philanthropy and public policy making. *Educational Policy, 14*(1), 11-24.

Holmes Group. (1986). *Tomorrow's teachers.* East Lansing, MI: Author.

Howard, R. D., Hitz, R., & Baker, L. J. (2000). Adequacy and allocation within higher education: Funding the work of education schools. *Educational Policy, 14*(1), 145-160.

Johnson, J., & Immerwahr, J. (1994). *First things first: What Americans expect from the public schools.* New York: Public Agenda.

Kettlewell, J. S., Kaste, J. A., & Jones, S. A. (2000). The Georgia story of P-16 partnerships. *Educational Policy, 14*(1), 77-92.

Mason, S. F. (2000). Do colleges of liberal arts and sciences need schools of education? *Educational Policy, 14*(1), 121-128.

Mitchell, A. H., Castenell, L. A., Jr., Hendricks-Lee, M. S., & Mooney, T. (2000). Balancing the politics of two cultures: Cincinnati Initiative for Teacher Education and the Cincinnati Professional Practice Schools Partnership. *Educational Policy, 14*(1), 107-119.

Murray, F. B. (2000). The role of accreditation reform in teacher education. *Educational Policy, 14*(1), 40-59.

National Commission on Teaching and America's Future. (1996). *What matters most: Teaching for America's future.* New York: Author; Teachers College, Columbia University.

Orfield, G., & Ashkinaze, C. (1991). *The closing door: Conservative policy and black opportunity.* Chicago: University of Chicago Press.

Recruiting New Teachers. (1998). *The essential profession.* Belmont, MA: Author.

Scannell, M. M., & Metcalf, P. (2000). Autonomous boards and standards-based teacher development. *Educational Policy, 14*(1), 61-76.

Smith, F. (1986). *High schools admission and the improvement of schooling*. New York: New York City Board of Education.

Thiessen, D. (2000). Developing knowledge for preparing teachers: Redefining the role of schools of education. *Educational Policy, 14*(1), 129-144.

U.S. Department of Education. (1997, June). *Excellence and accountability in teaching: A guide to US Department of Education programs and resources*. Washington, DC: Author.

USA Today/CNN Gallup Poll. (1996). *USA Today*, January 22, p. 6D.

Yinger, R. J., & Hendricks-Lee, M. S. (2000). The language of standards and teacher education reform. *Educational Policy, 14*(1), 94-106.

Contributors

Jerry D. Bailey is the director of the Institute for Educational Research and Public Service in the University of Kansas School of Education. He is the state of Kansas' copoint person in its partnership with the National Commission on Teaching and America's Future. A former public school teacher, counselor, principal, and associate dean for teacher education, he now works with projects dedicated to educational equity and opportunity. He also teaches graduate and undergraduate courses in education. His doctoral degree is from the University of Tennessee.

Larry J. Baker is the interim dean of the College of Education, Health and Human Development at Montana State University–Bozeman. He has a faculty appointment in the Department of Education in the Adult and Higher Education Program. His experience and academic interests are in the areas of legal issues, policy studies, and financing of higher education.

Louis A. Castenell, Jr., Ph.D., is a professor and dean of the College of Education, University of Georgia. He was dean for the past 9 years at the University of Cincinnati's College of Education. He is actively involved in promoting partnerships across campus and communities. His latest publications are on leadership and diversity.

Linda Darling-Hammond is Charles E. Ducommun Professor of Education at Stanford University where she also heads the teacher education programs. She is the executive director of the National Commission on Teaching and America's Future, the blue-ribbon panel whose 1996 report *What Matters Most: Teaching for America's Future* catalyzed major policy changes across the United States to improve the quality of teacher education and teaching. Her research, teaching, and policy work focus on issues of teaching and teacher education, school restructuring, and educational equity. Among her extensive publications is *The Right to Learn*, recipient of the AERA Outstanding Book Award in 1998.

Penelope M. Earley, Ph.D., is a senior director with the American Associa-

EDUCATIONAL POLICY, Vol. 14 No. 1, January and March 2000 184-189
© 2000 Corwin Press, Inc.

tion of Colleges for Teacher Education. Her areas of research include federal and state education policy and governance, public policy regarding teacher education, and gender equity issues. She has served on a number of educational advisory boards including the NCES Consultative Committee on Title II Accountability; AASCU Commission on Teacher Preparation, Accountability, and Evaluation; Teacher Mentor Project; Project on Early Childhood Violence Counseling; and Coalition for Women's Appointments in Government. She has authored book chapters for the *Handbook of Research on Teacher Education* and for *Developing Language Teachers for a Changing World* as well as various issue briefs and journal articles. Earley teaches courses on politics of education and on public policy to master's and doctoral students at the University of Virginia. Her undergraduate degree is from the University of Michigan, her master's is from the University of Virginia, and her Ph.D. is from Virginia Tech. She began her career in education teaching English and social studies at a junior high school in Ohio.

Karen Symms Gallagher is a professor of teaching and leadership and dean of education at the University of Kansas. She is currently the chair of the Kansas Commission on Teaching and America's Future and a member of the Kansas Professional Teaching Standards Board. Her research interests include educational reform, federal and state educational policy making, and P-12 partnerships. She is the author of a book on school policy and has served on the editorial boards of *Educational Administration Quarterly* and *Journal of School Leadership*. She also teaches the introduction to teaching course for KU's 5-year teacher education program.

Martha S. Hendricks-Lee is a research associate at the University of Cincinnati College of Education. Her research interests include systemic educational reform from prekindergarten through the doctoral degree.

Randy Hitz is the dean of the College of Education at the University of Hawaii at Manoa. He has served as a dean since 1998. From 1990 to 1998, he was dean of the College of Education at Montana State University–Bozeman. He has written many articles on educational policy and has served on a variety of policy committees at the state and national levels.

Richard D. Howard is an associate professor and program coordinator in the Adult and Higher Education program at Montana State University–Bozeman. He teaches courses in higher education administration, educational research, and statistics. He is a past president of the Association for Institutional Research and has numerous publications that address the creation and dissemination of information to support postsecondary planning and decision making.

Sheila A. Jones is the associate director of the P-16 Initiative for the Board of Regents, University System of Georgia. Previously, she taught mathematics for 21 years at Douglas County High School, Douglasville, Georgia, a charter school of the University of Georgia's League of Professional Schools. During her years as a classroom teacher, she served as the school's action research coordinator and as an on-site facilitator to other league schools. She has presented extensively on school renewal, action research, and teacher leadership throughout Georgia, the nation, and Canada.

Janine A. Kaste is a doctoral candidate in language and literacy education at Georgia State University and a graduate research assistant for the P-16 Initiative at the Board of Regents, University System of Georgia. She is a former classroom teacher of 10 years for Grades 2 through 6 in New York and Georgia. Her research interests include teacher education, educational reform (national and international), diversity, and language and literacy.

Jan S. Kettlewell is the assistant vice chancellor for academic affairs at the Board of Regents, University System of Georgia, and the cofacilitator of the Georgia P-16 Initiative. Prior to this position, she served for 14 years as the dean of the School of Education and Allied Professions at Miami University in Ohio. She has spoken nationally and published extensively on educational reform, with particular focus on the co-reform of teacher preparation and schools and standards-based education. She serves as Georgia's point person for several national initiatives, including the American Association of State Colleges and Universities Teacher Preparation Accountability and Evaluation Commission, the National Commission of Teaching and America's Future, and the Standards Based Teacher Education Project of the Council for Basic Education and the American Association of Colleges for Teacher Education.

Sally Frost Mason is dean of arts and sciences and a professor of molecular biosciences at the University of Kansas. All of her graduate and undergraduate training and professional experience has been at large public research universities where she has taught introductory biology for more than 20 years. One of her strong interests as dean concerns the role of arts and sciences in teacher preparation, especially in the sciences and particularly at research universities.

Phil Metcalf is presently mathematics department chair at Wawasee High School in Syracuse, Indiana. He has been a visiting professor at Ball State University for the past 2 years. Also, Metcalf is a member and current chair of the Indiana Professional Standards Board. He has been a junior-high mathematics educator for 13 years and a high school mathematics educator for 13 years. He received his bachelor of science degree from Ball State University in 1970 and his master of science degree from St. Francis University in 1975. He is a member of the Indiana State Teachers Association (ISTA), the National Education Association (NEA), the Association of Teacher Educators (ATE), and the Association for Supervision and Curriculum Development (ASCD). He was a Board of Examiners member for the National Council for the Accreditation of Teacher Education (NCATE) and now serves on the Unit Accreditation Board of NCATE. He serves on the Board of Visitors for Butler University in Indianapolis, Indiana, and the Alumni Board for Teachers College and Alumni Council at Ball State University in Muncie, Indiana. He was a member of the Mathematics Proficiency Guide Writing Team for the Indiana Department of Education.

Arlene Harris Mitchell is an associate professor of literacy and associate dean for academic affairs in the College of Education at the University of Cincinnati. She was a reading teacher, department head, and curriculum coordinator in Pennsylvania. Her scholarship has focused on poetry and literacy and connecting families and schools. She has served in leadership positions for both the International Reading Association and the National Association for Multicultural Education.

Tom Mooney is the president of the Cincinnati Federation of Teachers, a vice president of the American Federation of Teachers, and a member of the Board of Directors of the Holmes Partnership. He is a nationally recognized leader in educational reform and the professionalization of teaching. He and the Cincinnati Federation of Teachers are active members in the Teacher Union Reform Network (TURN), which studies high-performing teacher unions.

Frank B. Murray is H. Rodney Sharp Professor in the School of Education and Department of Psychology at the University of Delaware and the director of the Center for Educational Leadership and Policy. He served as dean of the College of Education between 1979 and 1995. Currently, he is the president of the Teacher Education Accreditation Council (TEAC) in Washington, DC. Prior to that he was the executive director of the Holmes Partnership and was chair of the National Board of its forerunner, the Holmes Group. He was president and cofounder of the Project 30 Alliance, an organization of faculty in education and the liberal arts.

Marilyn M. Scannell has been the executive director of the Indiana Professional Standards Board since July 1994. Her former positions include coordinator for academic programs and coordinator of the Dwight D. Eisenhower Higher Education State Grants Program for the South Carolina Commission on Higher Education, coordinator for School/University Cooperative Programs for the University of Maryland, and various assignments with the American Association of Colleges for Teacher Education (AACTE), including director of finance and administration. Dr. Scannell is also a former Chapter I mathematics teacher for Lawrence, Kansas, Public Schools. She is a member of the Interstate New Teacher Assessment and Support Consortium Standards Development Advisory Group and serves on the National Council for Accreditation of Teacher Education's Executive Board. She received her Ph.D. in education policy and her master of arts in higher education affairs from George Washington University and her bachelor of arts in international relations from the American University. She has made numerous presentations about performance-based standards and assessments, professional standards boards, and state policy for teacher preparation and licensure throughout Indiana and at the request of national associations.

Dennis Thiessen is a professor in the Department of Theory and Policy Studies in Education at the Ontario Institute for Studies in Education of the University of Toronto. Previously he was an associate dean (1991-1996) in the Faculty of Education and an associate director of the Joint Centre for Teacher Development (a collaborative initiative between the Faculty of Education and the Ontario Institute for Studies in Education). His research and development interests include teacher development, school improvement, and educational change. In recent years, he has conducted studies in such areas as (a) the experience of immigrant students and teachers in diverse education settings; (b) school development—exemplary secondary schools across Canada, restructuring middle and secondary schools in Ontario, and change-oriented elementary, middle, and high schools in Ohio; (c) beginning teacher learning in an elementary (K-5) school in Toronto; and (d) leadership development through school improvement initiatives in elementary schools in Eastern Ontario. He has worked extensively in school-university partnerships at the local (e.g., Learning Consortium), regional (e.g., Regional Centre for Educational Support Services), and international levels (e.g., Urban Network for Improving Teacher Education, North America; Institute for Educational Development, Pakistan).

Robert J. Yinger is dean of the School of Education and a professor of Educational Psychology at Baylor University in Waco, Texas. His research interests are in the areas of professional education and standards and the role of universities in comprehensive educational reform. He has published widely in the areas of professional knowledge, teacher cognition, teacher education, and professional standards. He received his Ph.D. from Michigan State University in 1977 and has held appointments as a professor at the

University of Cincinnati, visiting professor at Stanford University, distinguished scholar at the University of Alberta, and noted scholar at the University of British Columbia and the University of Hong Kong.